Breaking through Barriers
to Boys' Achievement
developing a caring masculinity

Gary Wilson

Continuum International Publishing Group

The Tower Building
11 York Road
London SE1 7NX

80 Maiden Lane
Suite 704
New York NY 10038

www.continuumbooks.com

First published 2006
Reprinted 2007 (twice), 2008, 2011 (three times)

ISBN: 978-1-85539-211-3

Managing editor: Janice Baiton – Janice Baiton Editorial Services
Cover design and layout by: Marc Maynard – MM design

Printed and bound in Great Britain

Contents

Barriers

Preface

The debate has raged for some time as to what the causes of boys' underachievement are. For long periods of time the debate centred around teaching and learning styles and/or the so-called 'laddish' culture. I believe that both are contributory factors, but my work has led me to conclude that there are around 30 significant reasons why some boys become disaffected, fail to perform and, subsequently, do not come anywhere near fulfilling their potential. This book invites you first and foremost to identify what the barriers to boys' learning are. You are then invited to look more carefully at particular boys, groups or classes, subject areas or Key Stages in order to identify which of the barriers outlined have a specific impact on the boys with whom you work. No two boys or groups of boys are the same, and it is vital that we approach the subject knowing that there is no quick fix. What you will find here is the benefit of my experience and also successful practice from a range of other sources that may well help. Most importantly, you will find an approach that has at its heart the desire to ensure that whatever we do to help our boys, we always have in the forefront of our minds the need to turn out decent young men and create what I care to call 'a caring masculinity'.

Gary Wilson
www.garywilsonraisingboysachievement.com

Acknowledgements

Acknowledgements to:

Diana, Martha, Ben and Zoe
Kirklees LEA
Sir John Oldham
Lorrin Campbell
The National Primary Care Development Team (The Improvement Foundation)
SAPERE
Susan Ainscough (Vital Connections)
Debbie Sanderson OBE, Jude Slack and Donna Sherwin (Mitchell High School, Stoke)
Sandra Smethurst
Jill Wallis
Christopher Marsden
Colin Noble
Wendy Bradford
Jerry Brown
Pat Holderness
Almondbury High School
Crosland Moor Junior School
Meltham Moor Primary School
Westborough High School
Royds Hall High School
Colne Valley High School
Chickenley Junior Infant and Nursery School

And all schools and teachers quoted within the text for their generosity and committment.

The author and publishers would like to thank the following for permission to reproduce copyright material:

Network Continuum Education (pages 20–21; four-stage cycle pages 54–55, 59–60)
Tony Ryan (page 27)
Kirklees Metropolitan Council (pages 97, 106, 119)
Department of Health/National Healthy Schools Programme (pages 99, 111)
Kirklees Learning Services (page 116)

Introduction: setting the context

Evidence and speculation abound as to the issues for boys' and girls' pre-school development.

Neurologists tell us many things. For example, that the quality of interactions during the first year of life can be a huge determinant of success; that early adversity encountered in the home can have a direct impact on neurological development; that while these impact on all children, there is a tendency for boys to be more sensitive to stress in their early years.

Psychologists tell us that when most girls start to use language, they use it co-operatively (and many would argue, they continue to do so for the rest of their lives); that most boys begin using language competitively (and, again, many would say that there is a tendency for a lot of men to continue to use language in this way!); that the female of the species is more prone to being an empathizer, while males are more motivated by and tend to engage with systems and are often dubbed 'systemizers'.

Statistics related to pupils with special needs are indeed quite alarming if you are the parent of a boy. The risks of developing any one of a series of conditions are significantly greater if you are male.

Higher risk conditions for males

Condition	Ratio
Dyslexia	3:1
Traumatic brain injury	2:1
Tourette's syndrome	3:1
Autism	4:1
Asperger's syndrome	10:1
ADHD	9:1
Conduct disorder (CD)	3:1
Note: 90 per cent of recidivist delinquents had CD at age 7	

What may be regarded as innate and what is not, however, is not the business of this book. This book investigates boys' experiences of school, the barriers to many boys' achievement and how to break such barriers down. It must be stated right from the outset that this does not apply to *all* boys. Indeed, many would argue that in some respects there are greater differences among groups of boys and among groups of girls than between them. This book focuses upon the experiences of a significant number of boys that are preventing them from gaining the kind of success that they are capable of and that they deserve.

Let us begin from the very first round of assessments that we make of children in schools – the Foundation Stage Profile. Starting from 2004, five year olds were measured in 13 different ways. The results of these assessments for the first two years are presented in the table opposite.

Foundation Stage Profile: % of pupils who have met or who are working beyond Early Learning Goals

Assessment	Girls	Boys
Disposition and attitudes	65	52
Social development	53	42
Emotional development	59	46
Language for communication and thinking	52	42
Linking sounds and letters	38	28
Reading	40	32
Writing	35	23
Numbers as labels and for counting	54	50
Calculating	39	36
Knowledge and understanding of the world	48	47
Physical development	66	54
Creative development	52	35
Shape, space and measure	45	41

Girls, as can be seen, are already ahead in every area – most surprisingly to some, as will be discussed later, in the area of physical development. The smallest gap, in knowledge and understanding, is perhaps rather less surprising, bearing in mind the acquisitive nature of many boys and their love of 'transportable' knowledge.

So into Year 1, where the cry is often heard 'But there's no sand! ... and the work's too hard.' (Of course we have 15- and 16-year-old boys who would just love to have that little tray of sand on their table to 'broddle' about in – and if you take that lump of Blu-tack out of that boy's hand, you may as well remove his brain – it is what he needs to help him concentrate.)

By the end of Year 2, boys nationally are being outperformed in every subject they are assessed in.

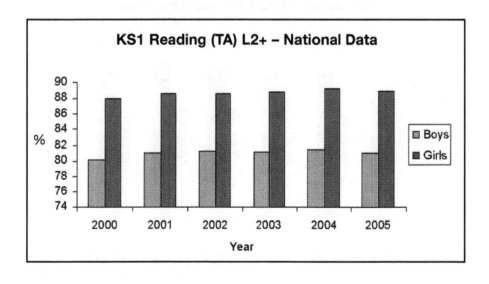

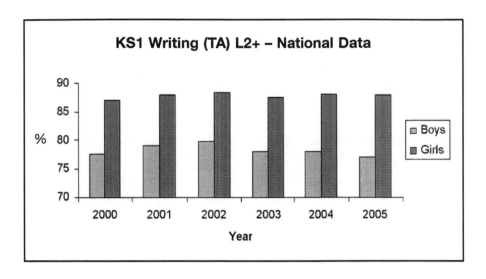

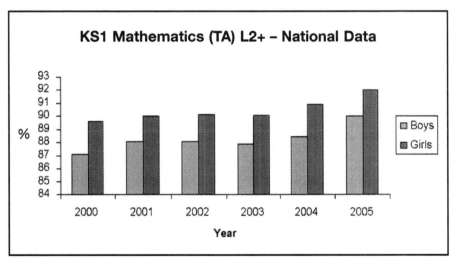

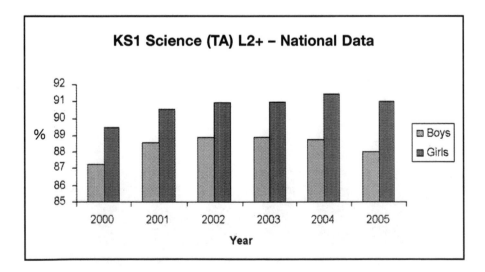

By the end of Key Stage 2, some ground has been made up in mathematics, but girls still outperform boys in English and science. Most notable are the differences in English, which, when broken down, amounts to a difference of around 6 per cent on average in recent years in reading, while the gap in writing is around three times that. Primary schools' concerns about boys and writing are clearly well placed as are the concerns about literacy at the point of entry to high school.

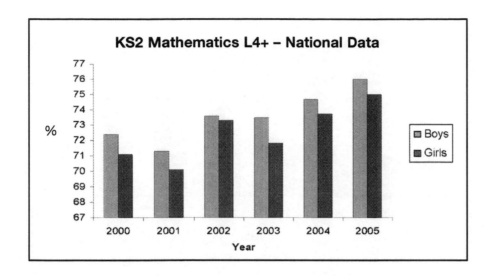

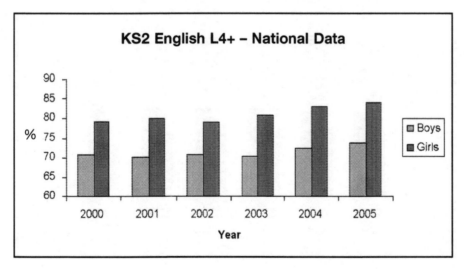

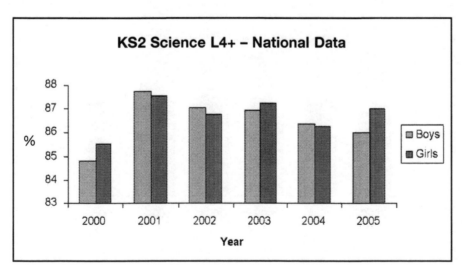

At Key Stage 3 there continues to be a pattern of girls outperforming boys that again, year on year, is not going away.

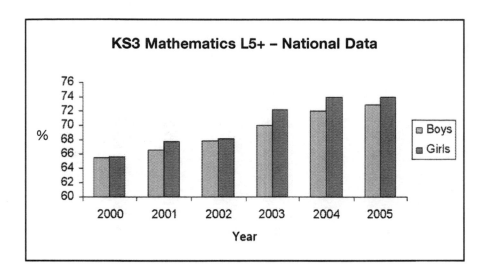

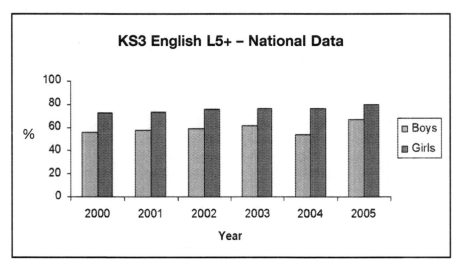

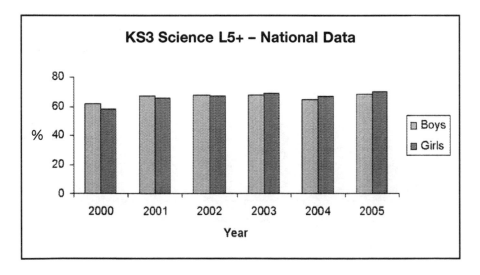

Once more, the largest gap is in English. By GCSE level, boys are being outperformed at A*–C in every subject.

Such a gap in language-based subjects is understandable, bearing in mind the differences shown in reading, writing and English in Key Stages 1, 2 and 3. Modern languages has an even bigger burden it might be argued: trying to persuade many boys that they should learn French – 'Why should I do that then? I'm not gonna live in France, and I can't stand Arsenal!'. Add to this the fact that there is a strong tendency to swiftly set students in high schools in this subject, meaning that often three-quarters of the top set are girls and three-quarters of the bottom set are boys. The size of the gender gap in subjects such as design technology is clearly, at least in part, because of the literacy content, as we shall explore later. By the time students get to A level, while girls in the 1970s were being outperformed by boys, the situation is now reversed. In recent years, around 58 per cent of entries to university were girls and there are now more young women in management training colleges.

The only two statistics that show boys to be in the lead concern permanent exclusion, currently above 80 per cent, and membership of the prison population (under 25s), which stands at around 90 per cent. There are also more suicides among young men today.

So what do we do? To begin we need to fully understand the reasons why this is happening in the first place. There is no single cause – try as hard as many commentators, the media and even some educationalists may to find one. Indeed, I believe there are around 30 barriers to boys' learning, some of which are perhaps more significant than others. Crucially, just as all boys are not the same, cohorts of boys and, of course, schools also differ. To this end, I believe that is vitally important that schools begin by examining carefully what the full range of barriers to boys' learning are. Subsequently, and by utilizing this book, schools can identify those barriers that are specific to their circumstances, be it a particular year group or class, Key Stage or subject area. After offering you a full exploration of the barriers, this book provides a grid to enable you to undertake a closer analysis and then begin to make an action plan with some of the strategies provided.

Just as there is no single, straightforward cause, neither is there a simple, straightforward answer, or quick fix. Subsequently, you will find here a wide range of strategies, many of which, it is hoped, will fit your circumstances. Good hunting! One key for all schools, I believe, is to ask the boys themselves. They know exactly why they are doing less well than the girls and many of them know exactly what they need to do about it too. Perhaps, above all, engaging boys in the process in this way shows them that you are ON THEIR CASE. A mega strategy if ever I met one!

I believe that it is vital to engage girls in the process too. If you are beginning a project on raising boys' achievement, it cannot be something you just work on secretly for boys, creating a project that you deliver at the boys solely for the boys' benefit. The benefit will be for everyone. If we spend time on addressing the attitude, behaviour and subsequently the performance of disaffected boys, then girls will clearly benefit. Who is it in many classes that demands most of the teacher's attention and uses up most of the teacher's time? Who is it in many classes that behaves in ways that are often antisocial, anti-academic and detrimental not only to their own learning but also to the learning of others in the classroom – especially the girls. Furthermore, as girls have had to live with this for significant periods of time, they can invariably contribute insights and effective strategies, as explored later, that can help improve the situation.

Barrier 1

Lack of independence prior to starting school

Reception teachers will tell you that it is very common for boys to turn up at school for their first time significantly less independent than their female peers. Sitting in the cloakroom after PE, underneath their pegs adorned with a little picture of a tractor or truck, many boys are quite content to allow the girls in their class to fasten their shoelaces or do up their shirt buttons for them. At the end of the day, boys are frequently to be found standing with arms akimbo. Why? They're waiting to have their coats put on. The most extreme example I have come across was at a school in Scotland where a boy, a few minutes into his first day, asked to go to the toilet. Twenty minutes later he reappeared, trousers around his ankles. Standing in the doorway, he called out to his teacher 'Who wipes the bums around here?'. Funny? Not really. Disturbing? Pretty much so. Learned helplessness? Almost certainly. We have to get messages to parents about the significance of encouraging the development of independence in young boys. If we do everything for our boys, we disable them, of that there is little doubt. It is clearly important that we plant the seed in parents that there is a strong link between developing independence and becoming an independent, and therefore more effective, learner.

As part of our work on teaching and learning we decided to survey all of our 9- and 10-year-old boys and girls. There were 29 girls in total and 40 boys. One question on the questionnaire was 'Who is responsible for YOUR learning?'. Every single one of the girls put that they were responsible. Out of 40 boys not a single one put that they were responsible for their learning ... they put the teacher, the headteacher, their parents.

First school headteacher

Within some cultures it is considered anathema to give young boys responsibilities; indeed, it is considered totally appropriate to do everything for them. As part of an ancient cultural tradition, it is not for us to judge or criticize. However, it is always, I believe, important that teachers communicate to parents just how powerful the link is between being an independent human being and being an independent and effective learner.

Pre-school providers, child minders, private nursery owners all have a significant role to play in ensuring that these messages are promoted when in contact with families. Pre-school home visits are opportunities to emphasize the importance of independence. Lists of 'can do' tasks for all parents' reference are widely used. Life-size cut-out models at the entrance to nurseries and Reception classes with cartoon speech bubbles quoting what independent tasks Ben and Martha can do now, can be useful in further promoting the message. Leaflets for home highlighting expectations can also be useful.

There can be no better strategy, however, than holding sessions with parents that specifically focus on how they might support their boys' development, not only in terms of developing independence but also in a range of other ways.

Barrier 2

Less developed linguistically on entry to school

All the evidence points to the fact most girls have more fully developed language skills before they even start school. Perhaps the most daunting statistic in this area is that, according to research in America in the 1990s, girls by and large appear to have superior listening skills before they are even born. Not much we can do about that then! There are areas where we can, however, make a difference.

Alarm bells have begun to sound in recent years via Ofsted reports and subsequent newspaper headlines declaring that the 'grunt culture' is now among us. It is very clear to everyone in the early years of education that the 'grunt culture' refers particularly, if not exclusively, to boys, many of whom are starting school less and less capable of articulate speech as time goes by. I recently visited a school where I was told that they had a handful of white working-class boys starting school each year, believing their names to be 'son', as they never hear their names. The same boys are also incapable of speaking in sentences. It is shown that girls use between 10 and 30 times as much language in their play even before school. A cursory glance at any nursery, infant or junior school playground shows that while many boys might be charging around being their latest action heroes, or kicking a ball (or each other!), many girls will be standing around in groups keeping the oral tradition alive. I am not being facetious here, I mean clapping games, rhyme games, skipping games or standing next to an adult so they can have an intelligent conversation.

And, of course, being linguistically less developed does not just mean that boys have a tendency to do less well in reading and writing SATs tests and language-based subjects through school, but it also clearly has a fundamental impact on the ability to express emotions and the subsequent development of emotional intelligence.

> Because girls develop facility with language more quickly than do boys, this leads them to be more experienced at articulating their feelings and more skilled than boys at using words to explore and substitute for emotional reactions such as physical fights.
>
> Boys for whom the verbalization of affects is de-emphasized, may become largely unconscious of their emotional states, both in themselves and in others.
>
> Girls become more adept at reading both verbal and non-verbal emotional signals, at expressing and communicating their feelings and boys become adept at minimizing emotions having to do with vulnerability, guilt, fear and hurt.
>
> *(Brody and Hall 1993)*

Put simply, a Reception teacher explained to me the link that she frequently saw between language development and behaviour.

> If he can't talk, he can't negotiate. If he can't negotiate, then he can't ask for what he wants. If he can't get what he wants, he grabs it.

While the majority of the barriers to boys' achievement can and do transcend ethnicity and social class, the barrier of linguistic development clearly does not. Recent research in the United States, for example, suggests that there is a huge difference in language development between social classes (Hart and Risley 1999). The study shows, for example, that a three year old in a middle-class family has an equivalent vocabulary to an adult from a 'welfare family'. It is clearly an issue that professional parents speak more than 1,500 more words per hour than those of unemployed parents.

In terms of emotional development, there is significance in the fact that the children of professional parents received 700,000 words of encouragement and 80,000 negatives, while children from parents on benefit heard 60,000 words of encouragement and 120,000 negatives. Since neurologists tell us that boys are more sensitive to stress and adversity in the early years of their development, there is obviously potential for boys to suffer most because of the lack of approval in the home environment.

Clearly, there is significant cause to help and advise pre-school providers, child minders and, above all, parents on the importance of developing language prior to starting school.

On one parents' evening in a relatively poor area in north-west England, I made my usual points about how only about half of the homes in this country now possessed tables around which families sit and eat. I pointed out that in countries such as France and Spain there are significantly less problems with oracy. I also recounted my horror at discovering that within one large town in England, membership of the library among under-fives amounted to approximately 75 per cent girls. 'Now that's not the boys' fault is it?' I posed the question: 'Why is that? Are parents saying – he's a boy, he won't be interested in reading? Or, he's a boy, he'll only misbehave and show me up?' At the end of the meeting a mum came up to me and said the following:

> That was really interesting what you said about reading and that, our Marcus (who was six and swinging on the hall curtains as she was speaking to me), our Marcus has been saying can he join the library like, he's been saying it for a year, and I've been saying 'no you blooming well can't' – I've been using it as punishment like, you know. But bearing in mind what you said, I think I'm gonna let him join. And that thing you said about tables, our Marcus has been saying for ages, 'can't we have us tea round the table' and I've been saying 'no, you'll have it on your blooming knee, in front of t'telly like everyone else'. But bearing in mind what you said, I think we might just start doing that.

For a start, it made me feel that turning out that night had been worthwhile for at least one of the nine mums that attended, but above all, it made one thing very clear: we have children in our schools as young as five or six, possibly even younger, who know more about what is good for them than their parents do. We have to get the messages to parents about the huge role they have to play in engaging boys in language-based activity if we want to reduce this particular barrier to boys' achievement.

Barrier 3

Forced to read and write before being physically or emotionally ready

There is only one country in the developed world where boys' underachievement is not a problem. Of all the Organization for Economic Co-operation and Development (OEDC) countries in 2004, for example, it came:

- second only to Hong Kong in maths
- top in science
- top in reading (the UK came eighth, fourth and seventh, respectively).

In addition in this country:

- school begins at seven with a focus on literacy
- there is very little setting or streaming – even in maths
- there are significant numbers of male teachers in primary school
- they do SPECTACULARLY better with those of average and below average ability.

Where is this? Finland. The subjects of setting and streaming, and the number of male teachers in primary schools will be covered later. Let us now consider how significant the starting age might be. I believe that it is hugely significant. Indeed, my top tip for ensuring that we continue to see girls outperform boys all the way through the education system would be: continue to force boys to read and write before they are mentally and physically capable. In this way, we would continue to give them an early taste for failure from which many of them will never recover. Not least of the problems this creates is that for many their handwriting style is born from a painful, ill-fated attempt to use the fine motor skills that have yet to be sufficiently developed. Many will spend their entire time in school unhappy about their inability to present their work to their teachers' satisfaction. If by the age of 11 they are beginning to get over the sense of being a failure, then what we could do to further instil it is to strictly set them. For the best effect, do this the moment they arrive at high school, and tell them that the system is a flexible one. They might believe in the system, and themselves, for a while, but not for long!

For children prior to the age of seven, there is a well organized kindergarten system in Finland and lots of structured play. The focus on literacy that occurs at the outset of formalized school is because they clearly believe that unless you can read and write you cannot access the rest of the curriculum. Hardly rocket science! Indeed, Finland is a hugely literate country. If you want to watch TV, for example, you have to read, as all programmes are shown in their original language with subtitles. Early literacy is also considered to be very important – but not too early!

Whenever I talk to five- and six-year-old boys about writing, the comments I frequently receive are not so much about how writing is boring or about how they would prefer to be out and about doing other things or that they struggle with subjunctive clauses(!), but rather about how they hate it 'because it hurts'. Many boys at the age at which we currently feel inclined to teach them to write are still developing the strength in their torso that will allow them to throw a spear at a mammoth! For many boys the development of fine motor skills comes much later.

 box

A group of 12 Year 4 boys were asked the question 'Do you like writing?'. The following are a sample of the answers they gave:

- 'No, it hurts your arms.'
- 'No, I'm rubbish because of my handwriting.'
- 'No, because my hand gets really sore.'
- 'I don't want to write.'
- 'You don't like getting spelling wrong – because it makes it rubbish.'
- 'No, because of my hand hurting.'
- 'Writing hurts my hand.'

Steven Biddulph, in his talks on raising boys, often refers to the suggestion that perhaps a better arrangement for schools might be having classes in which the boys are a year older than the girls, based on the fact that by about the age of nine there can be as much as a year's gap in terms of development between many girls and boys.

Research shows that if girls are going to underachieve, they usually start showing the signs at about Year 4. If boys are going to underachieve, the chances are that this will start much earlier, probably about Year 1. A reaction to the 'too much, too soon approach' to developing literacy perhaps?

Barrier 4

Playtimes for boys tend to be hyperphysical and 'boysterous'

Some time ago I encouraged a group of children in a primary school to perform a piece of research in playground behaviour. What these young researchers found and subsequently discussed with their school council was that boys were by and large charging round, often aimlessly and almost invariably engaged in some kind of activity with a ball, while girls, as discussed previously, were using masses of language in their play. The same school council then discussed ways in which they could change the culture of the playground. They began by considering ways in which the playground might be made a calmer place, by looking at what kinds of activities they might introduce. A budget was set and a rota to hand out games and materials was established. All this, of course, was very much welcomed by the teaching staff, who not only recognized that the council had become newly invigorated as they had been given a meaningful focus for once, but also knew their lessons would benefit. Lunchtime supervisors, renamed 'Play Leaders' and trained in playground games, also helped to structure play. Zoning primary school playgrounds is now fairly common as are the provision of classrooms for board games and other activities. What schools find interesting with the latter idea is the number of boys who choose to go to the board game room, who choose not to be out there on the 'killing ground' as someone once famously dubbed the school playground. Social areas in high schools can, of course, fulfil the same function very effectively.

We built a simple stage next to an outside wall in the playground. It was an instant hit with the girls. They started off by practising and performing dance routines. After a few weeks the boys decided they wanted in on this! It eventually developed into full-blown musical productions and plays, incorporating a soundtrack that had to be provided by a portable CD player.

Primary headteacher

The obvious implications of 'boysterous' activity at breaks in the school day are the problems of settling boys down to work afterwards. The competitive nature of their play can leave them in the kind of state that is hardly appropriate to learning.

Seeking to at once calm children down and take the macho edge off the start of school, many primary schools, and some high schools too, now effectively incorporate peer massage (as described on page 85) or breathing and relaxation exercises. Primary and high schools often incorporate quiet reading during tutorial time.

Various relaxation and gentle energizing exercises are becoming more and more popular as a way of calming children down and bringing them to a state of readiness to learn. To engage children most effectively, it is vital to ensure that they understand exactly why they are doing these exercises and what the effect will be. Subsequently, an introduction to left brain/right brain theory and a simple pre- and post-test should have the desired effect. One such test might be stretching down to touch your toes or, keeping the rest of your body still while moving your head gently from side to side. In both cases, post exercise, movement will have been improved as connectors from the brain to many parts of the body will have been invigorated.

An exercise intended to engage the brain in readiness for learning is sometimes called a 'lateralizer'. The more that is learned about the brain, and this is happening at a very rapid rate currently, it is clear that the corpus calossum, which joins the left and right hemisphere, does appear to be more developed in the female brain. Put simply, this means that the ability to make the connections between right and left and left as well as right hemispheres is easier for the female. Hence, some would argue, the ability of many females to multitask. The kind of exercises that involve cross-lateral movement and that wake up the connectors between left and right are therefore particularly useful for males. To this end, the following three examples from Alistair Smith's *Move It!* (2002) are the kind of 'lateralizers' that are useful, not only as part of creating the right learning state, but also for any part of the lesson when energy is dropping and brains are getting foggy!

Cross Crawler

With your right hand touch your left knee. Now with your left hand touch your right knee. Do it slowly and with big movements. Bring your knee up to meet your hand. Now try it with your elbows to your knees.

Morecambe and Wise

With your right hand go around your back and touch your left heel. Now with your left hand go around your back and touch your right heel. Do it slowly and with big movements. Bring your heel up to meet your hand. Now try alternate Cross Crawler with Morecambe and Wise.

Super Swapper

With your right thumb and forefinger pinch your nose, with your left thumb and forefinger hold your right ear. Now swap and swap again.

Gently massaging the ears from the tops down to the lobes two or three times can enhance listening capacity quite dramatically too, another useful situation to be in immediately prior to learning! This and many other Brain Gym® exercises can be found in the Brain Gym® books by Paul and Gail Dennison.

Having gone through a combination of the exercises above for the first time, a repeat of the toe touching or head turning exercise should convince the most cynical that something rather powerful and useful is happening.

It is now widely understood that readiness for learning is effectively enhanced by drinking water. But again, children need to be reminded that they are drinking the water because the brain is made up of more than 90 per cent water and that by the time we are thirsty a significant amount of brainpower (some say 20 per cent) is already lost.

An informal investigation conducted on the south coast by the National Healthy Schools team a few years ago showed that while pupils were increasingly being encouraged to drink water, it was often the staff that were in need of hydrating. They were the ones that never made time for a drink at breaktimes. They encouraged all staff in one Education Authority to drink a large sports bottle of water a day for a month. (Concerns about too many toilet trips were soon forgotten – the bladder does adjust quite quickly!) At the end of the month they noted a significant reduction in headaches and crabby behaviour!

Barrier 5

Many writing activities perceived as irrelevant and unimportant

> School for many boys represents a system of hostile authority and a series of meaningless work demands.
>
> *(Younger and Warrington 2003)*

> Over 60 per cent of writing undertaken in schools involves copying from books or from the board.
>
> *(NUT study)*

It is hard to find anyone who is not in broad agreement with Wendy Bradford's (2000) suggestion that 'Boys are the best barometers of good teaching'. Is it any wonder then that a fairly common response among boys to such activities as copying work from a board or from their books is 'Why should I copy that down? I've already read it.' Or 'Why should I copy that out? I know where it is if I need it.' Is it not the case that while many, if not most, girls in the classroom are massively 'biddable' and invariably engaged with work, many boys' responses to work in which they see no sense and purpose is that they just will not do it. Or at least they will not do it well.

> I will continue to work hard and do my very best, regardless of how pointless the task is.
>
> *Year 7 boy's self-evaluation on end of year report*

In order to engage boys effectively with their writing, I believe that it is possible to lay down a set of straightforward guidelines or rules.

Rule one: Are they given clarity of purpose and clarity of learning outcomes? As predominantly big picture thinkers, boys need to know not only why they are doing something, but also where it is leading and where it fits in with everything else.

Rule two: How engaging is the writing activity? For my part, I remember in years gone by attempting, as an English teacher, to wring some creative poetry from reticent adolescents and struggling. 'Imagine it's autumn. Imagine you're a leaf on the hill up there and a breeze catches you and brings you, whirling and twirling towards the school. And then you land, just here, outside the classroom window. How does it feel? Describe your emotions, describe the journey.' How did I engage anyone at all, let alone some great lumping 15-year-old boy?

Rule three: The potential for engaging boys is significantly increased if there is a clear audience for their work, rather than the teacher being the sole audience with the work doomed to join an ever-increasing dog-eared pile on the teacher's desk. If the work is a letter that is actually going to be sent somewhere, a story for a younger child, a PowerPoint for the school entrance hall, an email to a child in a feeder primary school, an article for a newsletter, a response to a newspaper article or a book recommendation for the library, then boys' engagement will be far more likely.

Rule four: Are they allowed time for reflection and, most importantly, discussion? I know, for example, that I would never have got those brilliant pieces of discursive writing about foxhunting if we had not had those lively formal debates. Neither would I have got those wonderful pieces of writing about the witches in *Macbeth* from those otherwise struggling Year 9 boys if I had not had that whole-class improvised court case where we tried the witches for their part in Macbeth's death.

How do I know what I think until I have heard what I said?

(W.H. Auden)

Rule five: Do they actually need to write it down? Hands up if you think that teachers do too much writing in school. Hands up if you do so much because you feel terribly accountable to fill up exercise books or wall space. Hands up if you sometimes even do writing as a means of control! Hands up if you think that writing less and concentrating on quality would be far better, especially for boys. All right, you can all put your hands down now.

Rule six: Is there a better format for writing it down? Do we look for huge chunks of continuous prose too often? If, for example, bullet points are acceptable in answering questions in end of Key Stage 3 English tests, why are they not good enough for other purposes? In terms of planning a piece of writing, mapping can be tremendously helpful for boys. Maps contain few words, are non-linear, provide a licence to be creative and allow a free flow of ideas that can later be organized in a straightforward fashion, such as through numbering.

Rule seven: Do they possess the skills to structure their writing? The simple answer is that many boys do not. Writing support mechanisms are often sorely needed (see next section).

Rule eight: Is it chunked down? Most boys feel what an eight year old recently told me, 'Writing in small amounts is best.' High schools, for example, where they have seen major improvements in the quality of their coursework have worked in 'boy-friendly chunks'.

> Like all geography departments, we used to set coursework in October and expect it to be in completed in February. When were lots of boys starting that then? February ... or March! We started setting it a chapter or section a month. We told them exactly what the criteria were and at the end of the month we collected in the work, gave feedback as quickly and in as much detail as we could, then moved on with the next section.
>
> *Geography teacher*

Rule nine: Is the feedback fast and useful, and do we as teachers show how much we value their work? Many boys respond badly to a 'score', feeling that below a certain level they are a failure and they become demotivated. A score and a comment frequently have the same impact. Boys just look at the score and ignore the comment, regardless of how useful it might be. What is most appreciated is the genuine interest of another human being, in the form of helpful written comment and positive encouragement or, preferably, in the form of verbal feedback. Another important element, specifically with creative writing, is the importance of gender neutrality in feedback. Do we only value description and not action, or even simply presentation rather than content?

Rule ten: Is there a culture in your school that enables boys to take pride in their writing? Indeed, is there a culture in your school that allows boys to take a pride in anything that is expressive or creative? One of the keys with regard to celebrating writing is the normalization of the process. It certainly helps if everyone's work is displayed, extracts of everyone's work read out or if whole-class anthologies are produced. In these circumstances, everyone has a licence and no one can be humiliated by others. Many schools display, and subsequently encourage, 'the most improved writers'. It helps too if, from time to time, we show public appreciation for those elements of boys' writing that represent those characteristics in boys that we (sometimes secretly) love and admire – such as their quirkiness, their humour, their love of pace and action.

A very productive start to the process of improving boys' attitude to writing and their perceptions of themselves as writers is, of course, to ask them ... sometimes, as the poem illustrates, you do not even need to ask!

A selection of responses from a Year 10 questionnaire

Q: How are you at planning your writing?

A: I don't plan it.

Q: What's the best way of getting you to write?

A: Talking about it first.

Q: Do you like it when your teacher shares your work with the rest of the class? Reads it out? Puts it on display?

A: Only if I think it's good.

Q: Are there any subjects where you particularly don't like the kind of writing you are asked to do?

A: Science – copying out of textbooks is boring.

Q: What's the best way of turning you off writing?

A: Talking about my handwriting.

All those questions … (any sound familiar?)

'Right boys – time to write.'

Sir, do we <u>have to … again</u>?
Can't we just talk about it instead?
Sir, can I borrow a pen?
Can I have some paper sir?
I left my book at home last night.
How do you start?
How much do you have to write?
What if you don't finish?
Do you write on both sides of the sheet?
Does the spelling matter?
Does it <u>have to</u> be neat?
Do you <u>have to</u> copy out the question?
Can't we just have a rest?
My arm hurts sir, I've got cramp.
Do I <u>have to</u> copy it out in best?
Can I go and work in the library?
Can I do it on the computer instead?
Sir, do I have to read it through?
I know what it is I said.
You're not going to read it out are you?
I don't want it displayed.
What's it for? Does it count?
Is it part of our final grade?

Gary Wilson

Why did not the Primary Literacy Strategy significantly move boys on in terms of their writing? Surely the fact that it contained elements that were fundamentally important to boys should have guaranteed success for them. So what mitigated against its success? Well, until 2005 there was no focus at all on speaking and listening.

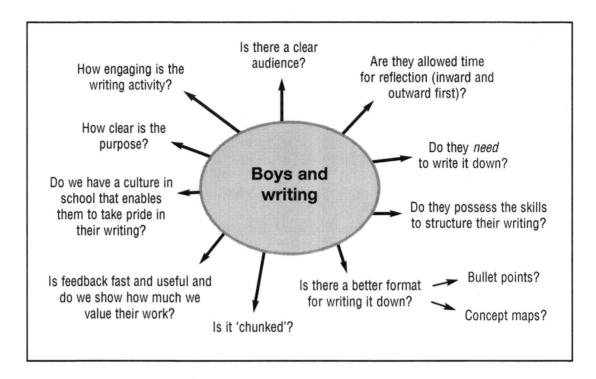

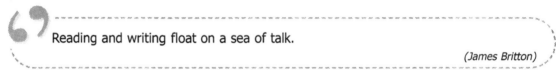

Reading and writing float on a sea of talk.

(James Britton)

As far as boys are concerned, all the research shows and all teachers instinctively know that boys REALLY need to talk through their ideas before they put pen to paper. Yet, according to a recent study, the average contribution orally to the literacy hour was three words.

Not a lot of words that. The overemphasis on grammar, might have, I suggest, clearly killed literacy stone dead for a lot of boys. Many are curious about language in the sense of enjoying looking inside a machine to see how it works, but this cannot be expected to engage and excite boys forever. The reduction of literature to a series of 'gobbits' (a fine old Yorkshire word I invented to represent a worthless chunk) did not help. Taking a chunk out of a book, throwing the book away and attempting to engage interest in the chunk did not work for many boys! As this removed real books from the menu, it clearly did not enhance the development of interest in reading fiction that is so critical to enhancing boys' learning either. The overemphasis on non-fiction, I would argue, has done boys very little good in terms of developing their ability to sustain concentration and reflect. At first sight, the literacy hour appeared to be exactly what boys needed, representing as it did, a chunking down of lessons. Perhaps, above all else, was the fact that it contained what is perhaps the most significant part of the lesson as far as many boys are concerned – the plenary. The plenary, however, by many teachers' admission, has not been as effectively and as widely used as it might have been. The importance of boys engaging in reviewing and reflecting on their listening cannot be underestimated, as will be explored later.

Subsequently, the Primary National Strategy (DfES 2005) has published a series of flyers for schools containing the following suggestions about how boys' writing might be improved.

'Talk for Writing' includes reference to the use of role play, drama, structured debates and the presentation of a persuasive argument prior to writing. Interviewing each other and members of the wider community are suggested, as is describing friends and family to others as starting points for developing characters. Also recommended is the use of response partners to evaluate each other's writing, thus using talk not only in preparation for writing but also as an integral part of the writing process itself.

The Reverse	The What If?	The Disadvantages	The Combination	The Alphabet
List things you would never learn in school.	What if there was no such thing as school?	What are some disadvantages of tests? How might they be overcome?	List what's good about a toyshop. Use these ideas to improve the design of a library.	Do an A–Z of things you can learn in school.
The BAR	The Variations	The Picture	The Prediction	The Different Uses
Use the 'Bigger Add Replace' strategy to improve displays around school.	How many different ways can you reward someone for doing well in school?	What connection has this picture with reading stories?	What would be the consequences if boys and girls were taught in different classes?	List as many different uses for an empty notebook as you can.
The Ridiculous	The Commonality	The Question	Mind mapping	The Inventions
What would happen if no one in the world could write?	What do books and teeth have in common?	The answer is a library. What are five questions that could have this answer?	Map out lots of ways to encourage people to work hard at school.	Invent a way of remembering your weekly timetable.
The Interpretation	The Brick Wall	The Construction	The Forced Relationship	The Alternative
Everyone will soon have to spend one hour a day learning a musical instrument.	Consider alternatives to working hard at school and getting a good job when you finish your education.	How can you plan your work out using a piece of string and some coloured clothes pegs?	How can using a computer make you a nicer person?	List ways of making people behave better without telling them off.

■ *Short speaking and listening 'warm ups' prior to writing. Using the self-explanatory headings, you can insert any appropriate phrases you wish. Adapted from* Thinker's Keys for kids *(Tony Ryan). Original (1990) and updated (2005) versions available for online download at www.tonyryan.com.au*

'Visual Texts' recommends not only the study of film sequences to extend writing on setting or dialogue but also the production of storyboards for film employing a range of text types. Video sequences or digital stills, from drama activities, for example, are also suggested as ways into writing openings or endings. With regard to the use of ICT, the recommendations include creating hyperlinked pages to make topic-based web quests or to create an interactive account of a visit. Web pages on particular interests are also recommended.

'Purpose and Audience' includes writing for younger children and writing instructions for making models or for a specific outdoor activity, which can then be evaluated and redrafted. Preparing a class anthology, articles for a school newspaper or book reviews for the school website are further recommendations. Also included are ideas related to the use of ICT, including the preparation of PowerPoint material to be used for a parents' evening and the development of email links for a joint geography topic. Persuasive leaflets and posters for display in the community are also suggested.

'Feedback on Learning' recommends encouraging boys to talk about what helped them to learn. It also recommends establishing response partners and creating 'golden rules' as to how these might operate. It suggests that teachers should model effective peer feedback and involve boys in drafting success criteria linked to the learning objective. Furthermore, it encourages actively engaging boys in peer assessment using success criteria.

Together these flyers represent a useful checklist of ideas and motivational techniques, and many of them, I would say, are equally applicable for all age ranges and in a range of subject areas.

Writing for young children was for me, as an English teacher for 28 years, one of the best things I believe that I have ever done. I miss teaching *Macbeth* (I taught it 27 times, I think), I miss teaching *Of Mice and Men* – because I used to cry at the end every single time I read it out loud and I thought that was good for me and my class – and I miss getting 15 and 16 year olds, boys in particular, to write books for small children. I remember their trepidation as they neared the nursery classroom to talk to the little ones about the kinds of stories they liked and to offer to write one for them. Their subsequent worry about the quality of the books they were going to write, knowing that they had to make sure that their hero worshipping audience were not disappointed. Their tremendous effort and concentration preparing the books, using their imaginations and their ICT skills to the full. I remember their palpable fear as I would load them into the minibus to take them down for that daunting launch of their new children's book. Then the total elation as they relaxed after the event, enjoying home-made biscuits and orange juice. Often, two weeks later we would hear that the nursery children had 'written' books for the 'big boys' and could they please come up and read to them now. The nerves would start flapping again, 'Oh no! Now we're going to have to make biscuits!' Basically, a win–win situation with boys being given a task with a real purpose, clear outcomes and a very real (and lively) audience, which gave them very real and invariably very positive instant feedback. For many there was the small matter that it utilized their not insignificant ICT skills.

The real experts though are the boys themselves, of course. Below are the suggestions of a group of nine and ten year olds, given on a one-to-one basis at a meeting of myself, teachers and pupils as part of a primary learning network meeting focusing on raising boys' achievement in writing.

'Be more persuasive,' says one eight year old. 'If you can't get me to write, then be *more persuasive*.' As for the boy who suggested that writing in small amounts is best – that was his idea, nobody told him about boy-friendly chunks! And as for the last one!

Top Tips for Teachers

Supplied by pupils from Marsden Junior School

✓ Choose the right time of day – not when we are excited after lunch/playtime
✓ Don't criticize if you can't read it – handwriting is not always the most important thing
✓ Talking stories can be good instead of writing them down
✓ Boys don't always want to be worrying about the spelling
✓ If I talk it through – I can say more on paper – I can also hear if it's boring and if it needs more detail
✓ Some of us are better at typing than writing, it's good when you can type up the final version
✓ It's good to get us to try different things out

Top Tips for Teachers (continued)

✓ Quiet reading calms us down
✓ Be more persuasive!
✓ Read more books together to get ideas for stories
✓ Looking at pictures and posters gives us ideas sometimes
✓ Being read to helps us with stories and poems
✓ Writing in small amounts is best
✓ Let us write any way we want
✓ Read more books – more examples to show us how to write in certain ways
✓ Give us lots of encouragement
✓ Give us lots of ideas to start with, like story beginnings
✓ Let us act stories out – to find out what characters are really like
✓ Let us share ideas with each other
✓ Give us time to think and talk
✓ Use mind mapping to work out ideas
✓ Give us basic ideas for stories
✓ You start a story and let the children finish it
✓ Use lots of props like a treasure box, hats, pictures
✓ Find out what interests us
✓ Make it fun
✓ Blackmail (£5 is about right!)

The UKLA report *Raising Boys' Achievement in Writing* (2005) usefully employed boys' voices by researching initially into their attitudes towards writing and their perceptions of themselves as writers. This is a useful and clearly effective approach. Subsequently, interventions were made, utilizing predominantly drama and visual approaches.

Some key findings of the project include:

● The project has impacted not only on standards of boys' achievements in writing but also on teachers'/practitioners' professional development and capacity.

● The planning and teaching model with the integration of drama and/or visual approaches was successful in promoting marked and rapid improvements in standards of boys' writing.

● The sample boys' perceptions of themselves as successful and satisfied writers improved considerably as a result of the project. It has impacted not only on standards of boys' achievements in writing but on teachers'/practitioners' professional development and capacity (www.ukla.org/site/research).

What kinds of questions might you ask your boys about writing, prior to utilizing some form of intervention?

- What do you enjoy about writing?
- What kind of support/help would improve your writing?
- Which, if any, of the following do you find difficult?
  1 Coming up with ideas?
  2 Planning your writing?
  3 Coming up with a conclusion?
  4 Having to express your opinion?

Remember, if you are going to ask them to write answers in a questionnaire, at least give them the chance to discuss it first!

We will not improve boys' writing simply by doing more and more. However, we will improve it if instead we allow more time for talking and insist on less time for writing.

There is a fairly common misconception that computers provide a miracle cure for issues around boys' underachievement. It is known that computers engage and motivate many boys, but not necessarily for educational purposes. If a boy cannot write a story on a piece of paper, why should he suddenly be able to when placed in front of a keyboard? We cannot rely on computers alone to perform the raising boys' achievement miracle. If, however, we use ICT to address some of the specific barriers to boys' learning, such as their perception that most writing that they are asked to do has little real purpose, or is rarely for a real audience, then we might make a difference. Similarly, many boys respond well to an element of challenge in their work and their preferred learning styles mean that they can gain immensely from the broader definition of ICT outlined below. From my experience, I truly believe that *ICT does present tremendous opportunities to raise boys' achievement, if:*

- lessons using ICT are well planned, structured and have a clear focus with clear aims and objectives explicitly stated.
- teachers are clear in their explanations.
- teachers make good use of their reflective questioning techniques to ensure pupils consider such issues as how ICT is helping them in their learning.
- a plenary session is used at the end of the lesson to allow boys to reflect on what has been learned.
- used effectively to help boys structure their written work. Just because they are using a computer it does not mean they suddenly know how to structure their writing.
- used properly to develop research skills; for example, the correct use of search engines, alternative search engines, how to précis material and how to critically evaluate material (not just cutting and pasting from the internet).
- peer tutoring can be effectively employed.
- an element of challenge is introduced; for example, who can make the most creative use of the technology to improve presentation.

To help raise boys' achievement through the use of ICT we need to be:

1   Developing skills that currently are a significant barrier to most boys' learning by:

- employing significant use of discussion while learning
- using commercial packages to help boys develop their writing skills, such as Word Bar in the primary school, or teacher-prepared writing frames across the age range
- exemplifying the process of drafting work on the computer to ensure that it becomes a seamless process from first draft to final edit
- using commercial packages such as Inspiration and Emindmap to help develop boys' planning and preparation skills
- using devices that incorporate handwriting recognition, which are believed to encourage boys to improve handwriting and which enable them to get words into word-processed text easier and quicker
- working from their strengths by using voice recognition software to record, for example, verbal evaluations, and subsequently transform them into text
- using the full range of tools available on Word such as the outlining tool, highlighting tool or 'track changes'.

2   Providing boys with a real sense of purpose and a real audience by:

- setting up email links with a parent's workplace
- setting up email links with businesses for careers work
- setting up email links with other schools for cross-phase collaborative book writing, where high school students negotiate the content and style of a book that they are writing for a specific pupil in one of their feeder schools
- encouraging the use of email to work on collaborative homework tasks
- setting up email links with similar schools to write stories collaboratively; for example, writing alternate chapters – also adding here a sense of challenge
- publishing material on the school's intranet or on the internet
- the development of web pages incorporating videos produced by pupils explaining newly learned concepts and ideas
- lots of 'instant' publications such as anthologies, newsletters, newspapers, leaflets (short-term targets and short-term rewards)
- the production of web pages or an electronic newspaper using PowerPoint, as an enrichment or extension activity.

The popularity of 'Choose your own adventure' books with many boys can be used to good effect by getting them to create a PowerPoint story with hyperlinks leading to alternative choices of storyline (Social and Emotional Aspects of Learning (SEAL) materials contain a good exemplar 'Jack's Choice', see website www.standards.dfes.gov.uk/primary/publications/banda/seal).

Similarly, the popularity of photo stories in magazines can be re-created through PowerPoint 'storyboards'. Six PowerPoint slides on a page complete with speech bubbles actually look like a photo story.

Barrier 6

Difficulties with structuring written work

Many boys require help with structuring their written work. What they do not need, however, is a sterile, pre-prepared, off-the-shelf, one-size-fits-all writing frame. Just as many years ago pupils were suffering a slow and agonizing death by worksheet, the same fate awaits those pupils at the hands of the 'I've got a writing frame, and I'm damn well gonna use it!' teacher. Boys need engaging not only with the subject matter, the sense of audience and the learning outcome, but also with the writing process. Getting boys involved with looking at a variety of texts of the type that they are about to write themselves and being led towards an analysis of the good and bad features is a useful starting point. This process helps in terms of flagging up what elements to include in a successful piece of writing. Choosing subjects that interest them from which to draw exemplars will, of course, increase engagement. Teacher modelling the thought processes involved in planning a piece of writing out loud, and then writing it up LIVE, there and then on the OHP or interactive white board, is the only way to create a writing frame. In this way, the teacher is creating a frame that fits exactly with that particular activity on that particular day with that particular group of pupils. If the teacher delivers in a dull, flat way, so too will the pupils.

> " Modelling isn't just a good way of teaching someone how to do something – it's the only way.
>
> *(Einstein)*

I lost count of the number of times in almost 30 years of teaching I would hear the doleful 'How much do we have to write sir?' I used to say 256 pages – they would not ask again that lesson. To many boys, a blank piece of paper can seem to stretch out endlessly into the distance. As discussed earlier, the idea of developing pieces of writing a section at a time does suit many boys. Developing a strong introduction, as modelled by the teacher, before moving on has the added benefit of providing boys with short-term goals. Verbal feedback on the quality of their work, stage by stage, will also give them the short-term gratification that many need.

At various stages of their development as writers, the use of planning grids, paragraph headings and even sentence starters can provide the kind of support that boys need. Tight formal constraints can reduce the number of choices that boys have to make in the writing process and therefore give them that extra little bit of security many of them seek. Often, writing forms that present challenges to boys such as haiku or a mini saga (a story using exactly 50 words) can appeal.

If the piece, as many pieces of high school coursework do, requires a written evaluation, or at least a thoughtful conclusion, then this is again out of the comfort zone of many boys. The reflective processes that are required to elicit an evaluation, or even a simple conclusion, need constant rehearsal. Immediately prior to this stage of the writing, discussion – in pairs, in groups and then as a class – is the most effective way. The more actively engaged boys are in the discussion, the better their writing will be. If the teacher, and the pupils themselves, map out the ideas coming from the discussions, the result will be even better. A simple map, used on this occasion to note down a range of points, can be used to structure the final section of the writing with ease. Numbering the points on the map in the order in which they might be used in the conclusion provides a straightforward skeleton

The most potent tool for developing boys' ability to structure their writing from start to finish is to first of all create the structure orally.

 box

Guided visualizations

A guided visualization with a set of clear, time-linked instructions can suit many boys in creative writing. One example might be 'The Path of Life'. The teacher shows a slide of a forest path and allows, say, two minutes for each of the following instructions, more if necessary:

- You are walking along this forest path. Describe what you can see.
- As you walk along the path, you come across a tree that has fallen, blocking your way. Describe the tree using the rule of 3s (for example, brown, crumbly and moss covered).
- As you make your way over the fallen tree, you see something small and shiny in the grass. What is it? Describe it.
- Then your eye is caught by a dwelling in the distance. Describe what you see. Describe what you hear and what you can smell.
- Take a break – you are allowed to change three words that you have used that you are not happy with.
- Now carry on – complete the story.

Barrier 7

Reticence about spending time on planning and preparation

Mapping

The mapping of ideas is an extremely powerful tool for several reasons, many of which are related to planning and preparation. Maps enable us to:

- gather ideas together
- let our imaginations run free
- save time
- focus clearly on an issue or problem
- make clearer and better notes
- remember things and revise effectively.

Above all, the fact that maps allow boys to see the big picture is what makes mapping an especially powerful tool for boys. For most boys, the outcome of the planning process HAS to provide them with absolute clarity and a view of exactly where something is going. Without this many will fail to engage or soon flounder. Mapping gives boys that clarity and enables them to always see the big picture as they work through the process that follows. Maps also deliver this in a way that is not linear – a real bonus for boys. The fact that maps give them a licence to be creative adds tremendous value for them. They are also a massively efficient way for many boys to take notes. Day after day pupils are encouraged to take notes and, more often than not, the expectation is that the notes will be taken in a linear form. The brain prefers to store information by association, in a pattern, not unlike the pattern created by a map such as the one illustrated opposite. The more boys in particular work with this approach, the better it will be for them.

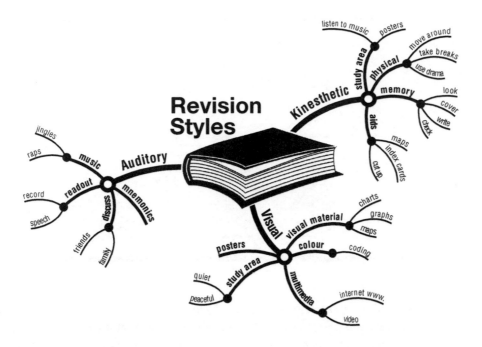

Organizing information

The use of graphic organizers to aid planning is also widely acknowledged as having positive benefits for boys. Venn diagrams, for example, are useful for sorting information by making comparisons between ideas, things, people and so on. The characteristics of two items being compared are listed in the largest segments of the circles and anything that is in common is written in the overlapping section. Comparing two poems that are being studied for GCSE in this way, for example, can help sift out ideas in preparation for writing a comparative piece.

Venn diagram

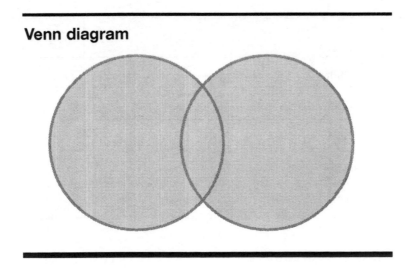

Fishbone diagrams are used to show the cause and effect of something, such as the Second World War. By adding as many fishbones as necessary, ideas can be sorted out and connections made prior to writing.

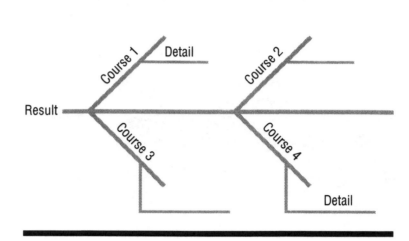

Plus, Minus and Interesting (PMI) charts can also help to sift and organize ideas. Pupils list plus points, minus points and points of interest on a simple chart that they then use to sift and organize ideas. Flow charts, like maps, are an excellent way of planning, organizing and remembering information that appeal to the big picture thinker.

The vital ingredient that has to be added to all of these and any other similar approaches is talk. Working through these processes with a partner will ensure a far better written outcome.

'Where do you stand?'

Getting boys off their seats and actively engaged in a physical way can help many of them clarify their ideas and bring themselves to a conclusion. The 'Where do you stand?' shown below (any statements can be used, related to the topic being studied) does just that.

		Agree	**Disagree**
1	Playing computer games is bad for boys.		
2	Using computers improves boys' writing.		
3	Mixed ability is the only way to teach English.		
4	Handwriting and spelling do not matter.		
5	It does not matter what boys read, so long as they read.		

1 Pupils circulate around the room, finding others who agree or disagree with the statements. They have to be able to briefly say why they feel that way, and then write the person's name in the box.

2 The question with the most evenly split responses is then chosen, by a show of hands.

3 Pupils are moved to either side of the room according to whether or not they agreed or disagreed.

4   Each of the two groups are asked to determine who feels most strongly about the issue and who feels least strongly.

5   The two groups are asked to line up in one line with those who agree most vehemently with their original position at either end of the line (the fence is in the middle!).

6   Select three pupils from each end of the line and hold a formal debate.

Developing boys' research skills using ICT

For many boys, it is possible that by the end of high school they will still think that researching means cutting and pasting something from the internet straight onto a blank Word document, sticking their name on the bottom and then just handing it in – without even reading it. That they have reached that point in their school career without having developed those skills is something that we have to address.

The following activity is useful for helping to develop boys' research skills using ICT:

1   Provide a list of ten appropriate websites of variable quality.

2   Pupils select the three most useful/appropriate and, using the highlighter tool, highlight them on the list.

3   They cut and paste extracts from each website onto a Word document.

4   Pupils select useful sections, using the highlighter tool.

5   They summarize or précis the information, and use quotes if necessary.

6   Examine the end result and the process.

The fact that many boys (and some girls) clearly lack the ability to effectively seek out information and make sense of it has to be put down to the fact that the teaching of information literacy is often far from satisfactory. Basic library skills delivered to Year 7 students as they arrive at high school are often the same as the ones delivered to Year 2 pupils. A report issued by Ofsted (2006) into school libraries found that:

● too many pupils struggle to make effective use of information

● the teaching of information literacy is rarely effective or coherent

● discrete information literacy programmes need to be balanced with research in real contexts, that is, links with all areas of the curriculum.

Just as there is a whole-school approach to ICT, it surely seems appropriate that there should be a whole-school approach to information literacy.

Barrier 8

Reading fiction perceived as a female province

Why is it that many boys feel that reading fiction is just something that women and girls do? It may well have been their experience that it was mum that read to them before they started school, either because it was perceived in the home that that is who should deal with that particular job or because there simply was not an older male there. It may also be partly because they never saw an older male in the house read and, if they did, chances are that they saw them read only a newspaper or an instruction manual. Therefore, their idea of why males read is that they read to find out, and therefore only non-fiction will do if you are male. It may also be the case that they never encountered a male teacher who inspired a love of literature in them until they reached high school. (Currently only 48 per cent of pupils have been taught by a male teacher prior to high school.)

Does it matter that they think this way? It certainly does. As a high school head of English, I decided many years ago that I simply had to get all boys to read. And to read fiction. The words 'teeth' and 'pulling' as well as 'stones' and 'blood' spring to mind in memory of that particular exercise. Why did I do it? Because I was sick to death of seeing them fighting over the *Whopping Great Big Book of Records*, then flicking from the back to the middle, then to the front, then three minutes later swapping it for the history of their favourite football team, then swapping THAT for something they had had read to them when they were four or five, such as *The Twits* or *The Magic Finger*, so that not only were they in their comfort zone, but also if the teacher came round, they could say 'Yes miss, I know what's happened in the story.' Nothing of any value had gone on there whatsoever. So I banned the use of non-fiction texts in the library during English lesson time. It took time, but the benefits were immense. As many teachers do at parents' evening, for years I would nod sagely when a parent said, 'It's hopeless getting him to read fiction, he reads fishing magazines – that's reading isn't it?'. Not any more. Why fiction? Boys need to read fiction because boys desperately need all the help they can get to help them REFLECT. The perpetual 'Whoppinggreatbigbookofrecordsflicker' is in danger of turning into the young adult who cannot focus or reflect on anything for long. In turn, his chances of becoming the adult male who cannot express his feelings or work out a measured response to a problem are potentially far greater. Reading is not just about improving spelling or building vocabulary, nor is it just about enhancing our ability to deal with punctuation. It is that and more, much more. It is about reflecting on emotions and relationships, characters and situations.

Engaging boys in fiction

How can teachers effectively support the move to engage boys in fiction, particularly in the high school? There are lots of ways. Talking to boys AND girls together, in the context of a school council, about the problems I had in persuading boys to read meant that they suggested creating a 'Boyzone' in the library. In this the front covers of books were displayed (far more interesting than that narrow bit down the side), together with a range of brief, attractively presented recommendations from other boys (better than reviews, which are too dry). We found that it helps if wall charts are presented imaginatively, showing who is reading what (boys versus girls).

Devising reading challenges and quests to engage and inspire helps, as can encouraging boys (and girls) to produce MTV-type short films recommending books that pupils can access in the library. Making the library alive by bringing in visitors who will engage children, such as authors, poets and theatre groups, is vitally important. On one occasion I brought in a 'Games Workshop' event, based on *Lord of the Rings*, using their beautifully crafted and painted models. Two young, bearded Games Workshop employees arrived with a huge board containing minuscule mountains and rocks and proceeded to re-enact the flight to the ford from the book. A short time into the activity I glanced round and realized that the boys gathered there were, without exception, the very brightest boys in school. I was intrigued to find out why.

I set up a lunchtime club so that I could chat to the boys informally about their interest. It soon became clear. The activity gave them a licence to be creative – you can spend a whole day painting one of those models and they often did. It also gave them a licence to get together to play socially with a hint of competition, but not the frenetic competition that fills many boys' leisure time. As far as serving my purposes were concerned, it also gave them a licence to be engaged with something that was literary and that involved a significant amount of literacy too (some of the role/rule books are thicker than an old London directory!).

Recently, there has been a tendency for boys to pick up on a book that is a particular hit and then, not knowing what to read next, just read the same book over and over again. The record for this particular activity I noted down was a young lad who had read his particular favourite 11 times. Guiding boys on their reading journey is a significant responsibility for teachers and librarians alike.

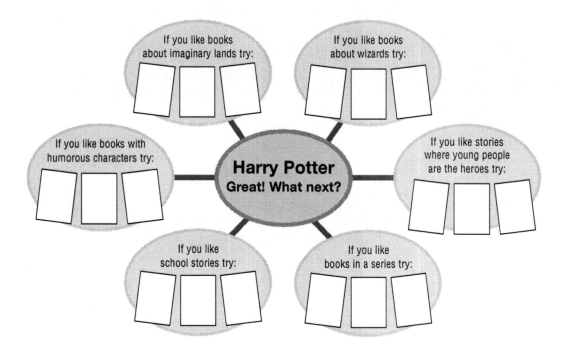

Promoting fiction

It is really important to promote reading around the school and the best people to use for this are not obscure television personalities, or even sportsmen – while they can help, I believe that many role models that have been used in the past exert a limited influence on boys – but, in my experience, it is far better to use your own peer leaders from within the school to promote positive learning behaviour. Furthermore, I would suggest that you make the posters really large – nobody takes a great deal of notice of anything less than A1 or 2 paper size. Pictures of your own male staff and ex-pupils are also recommended. Peer leaders, or the 'peer police' as I call them, can play a hugely significant part here.

One high school included 'The' Lad (not just one of the lads – but the lad) in its reading campaign. The boy was seen holding a suitable work of fiction and was used in an extensive poster campaign around the school. The fact that his picture was all around the place he thought was fantastic – the fact that he had never read a book in his life was largely irrelevant! Here he was, promoting positive learning behaviour. This effectively represents the issuing of licences to any boy who wanted to read and encouragement to any who might not previously have given it a second thought.

The use of imaginative displays can help. One I know of involved suspending a collection of exciting new books by popular authors such as Anthony Horowitz in a roll of barbed wire from the library ceiling. Accompanying this was a note saying 'YOU CANNOT BORROW THESE BOOKS UNDER ANY CIRCUMSTANCES!!' When a few weeks later it was announced that they would now be available for loan at such and such a time, there was a queue from the dining room to the library.

Info box

Many boys like books that:

- ✓ are plot driven
- ✓ have an edge to them
- ✓ are controversial
- ✓ are funny
- ✓ are about powerful ideas
- ✓ appeal to their sense of mischief
- ✓ are in a series
- ✓ reflect an image of what they would like to be.

But, most importantly, if you are going to add books to your library and you want boys to use them, then let boys help choose them.

Libraries are vital

Libraries are the first line of attack in engaging boys in reading effectively and should be the heart of any school. Unfortunately, for all kinds of reasons, this is not always the case.

- In too many schools, senior managers do not take a sufficiently close interest in the use of the school library or the impact it has on pupils' learning.
- Schools rarely ask librarians to report formally on library policy, use of resources and effectiveness.
- Librarians are rarely included in English department meetings.
- Schools rarely have an effective library development plan.

(DfES 2004)

Could it still be the case that some headteachers are quite happy so long as their library 'looks nice'?! One very useful question for a school to ask itself, rather than just bask in the glory of an attractive room full of books, would be: 'The school has a problem with boys' underachievement, what can the library do about it?'.

 box

Boys' underachievement: what can school libraries do?

Enthusiastically and imaginatively promote the reading of fiction through:

- creating a boy-friendly space in the library
- using imaginative techniques to present recommendations, such as pupil-produced, MTV-style videos, a PowerPoint loop featuring quotes from other boys and illustrations from books
- displaying posters featuring them and their peers engaged in reading
- developing a reading 'trail' or reading challenges, competitions and quizzes with prizes as incentives
- themed displays around 'books of the film'
- inviting male authors, poets, book illustrators to visit.

Engage boys in the life of the library by:

- involving them in the process of choosing and buying fiction
- giving them responsibilities within the library
- starting a boys' book club/chess club/philosophy club.

Sometimes boys just simply choose to use the library as a sanctuary.

I love the library
It's my special place
I love the library
It's warm and it's safe
I love the library
It's the playground I fear
I love the library
They can't get me here
I love the library
I love the way it looks
I really love the library
But I can't stand books

Gary Wilson

Continuity of provision of library services from primary to high school can be an issue too. If a primary school library environment that is exciting and engaging, that actively draws boys into it to get involved is followed by a somewhat duller and often significantly less engaging service in the high school, then this could effectively discourage boys. It is always a good idea for high schools to be aware of where their boy readers are (literally) 'coming from'. Cross-phase visits and the sharing of expertise can be extremely useful.

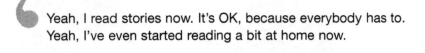

> School libraries can have a positive impact on academic achievement and the broader aspects of student learning, including motivation.
>
> *(DfES 2001)*

Reading Week

One successful approach I have instigated in many schools is a regular Reading Week. Not a new idea, but massively effective. Every half-term one week is chosen when everyone reads for one lesson each day throughout the week. The time of day changes on a rotation basis. The normal timetable is abandoned and everyone reads (fiction). The teacher reads, the caretaker reads and the office staff read. In one school, if a visitor arrives, they are handed reading material and asked to wait while reading ends. Apart from changing the entire atmosphere of the school extremely dramatically, it can have a massive impact on encouraging readers, not least because it normalizes the process but above all because it gives boys a licence to read.

> Yeah, I read stories now. It's OK, because everybody has to.
> Yeah, I've even started reading a bit at home now.

> I like this reading hour, it's enough good. People don't normally read, this way everyone reads. I didn't really read but I am going to do more 'cause I've enjoyed it.

> Through this school it's normally loud, but through this hour it is really quiet and everybody's relaxed – you get really into it. We would like it every day.

Early years reading

A few years ago I discovered that in one city the gender breakdown of under-fives who were members of children's libraries in the area was about 75 per cent female and 25 per cent male. This is not the boys' fault. What are the parents thinking? He's a boy, he won't be interested in reading, so I won't take him? He's a boy, I can't trust him not to misbehave and show me up, so I'm not taking him? Whatever the reasons, parents really need to be made aware of the importance of boys' reading, and reading fiction in particular.

Parents need to know that:

- joining the library is free and yet its benefits are priceless
- books make great presents
- talking to children's librarians or teachers can help give them ideas for what books to buy or borrow
- older males reading in the house really helps
- reading the same book as their son means they have the opportunity to discuss things they have never discussed before
- older males reading to boys as they grow is vital
- reading homework is just as important as any other kind
- stopping reading to your child at the point when he can read to himself is a mistake. Even high school students (and adults!) still get lots of joy from being read to.

There are now many books that can be recommended to parents and used in the early years of school that will serve an even wider purpose. Books that confirm girls to be caring, thoughtful and loving characters, while the boys portrayed are content to charge around the place without a care in the world are unlikely to help in the development of a caring masculinity. There are, however, a growing number of children's storybooks that serve to smash stereotypes and portray boys in caring and loving roles (see Appendix 2). The same books might be usefully approached in the high school as resources to examine the way in which positive stereotyping can be created.

Barrier 9

Teacher talk and teacher expectations: gender bias

> " The heart of the issue is the day to day relationship between teacher and pupil. The essential theme is that teachers must rethink the language they use when communicating with boys inside and outside the classroom.
>
> *(Peter Downes 2002)*

Midwives have informed me that there have been studies to prove what they have always noticed, which is that the very first moment a baby is handed to its mother there is a distinct difference between the way she speaks to her baby depending upon the sex of the child. If the baby is female, the hold is gentler and the voice softer. If it is a boy, the hold is firmer and the voice somewhat stronger. When I think back on 28 years of teaching, I am quite dramatically aware of the differences in the ways in which I have spoken to girls and boys 'That's lovely dear...' *'And what do you think you're doing!'*

 box

> ***What*** do you really mean?
> What ***do*** you really mean?
> What do ***you*** really mean?
> What do you ***really*** mean?
> What do you really ***mean***?
>
> *Communication:*
> Words chosen and used = 7%
> Tone of voice = 38%
> Non-verbal accompaniment = 55%

It is evident that what we are actually communicating has very little to do with the words we use and far more to do with our tone of voice, our body language and our general demeanour. When we are discussing issues around boys' achievement, it is extremely common to hear the following from boys:

It's because teachers favour girls, that's why.

Aye, and there's a lot more of them about these days an' all. When a boy does something bad then straight away he gets into trouble. Then I've seen girls do exactly the same thing and get away with it. It's just not right is it?

Girls are definitely teachers' favourites aren't they?

(Let's Hear It From the Boys)

For some time I thought little of it. Perfect excuse I thought, and I put it down to boys' aptitude for fancy footwork. The fact that it ALWAYS comes up forced me to rethink. Quite simply, a lot of boys just think that teachers do not like them. Exploring our attitudes to boys and girls as homogeneous groups does not sit comfortably, prone as it is to stereotyping. However, having asked numerous groups what they like about teaching girls and what they like about teaching boys, it has served to highlight some significant points. The following, unedited list, elicited on sticky notes from a group of primary teachers is a typical example.

What I like about teaching boys...

- Finding ways to turn them 'on' and harness all that energy
- They get stuck in
- They're lively
- They're interested in practical things
- They love facts
- They're fun
- They're upfront and honest
- They're adventurous
- Their sense of humour
- They ask questions
- Their enthusiasm
- Their energy
- Their sense of humour
- They can have more weird and wonderful ideas
- Every day is a new day – usually!
- Their liveliness and sense of humour
- Their enthusiasm when hit by something which really inspires them
- Their enthusiasm

- Their energy
- They're so direct
- The questions they ask
- Their humour
- They have a go
- They explore
- They often speak their mind – they're honest
- They're often more practical, although they need instructions in short, sharp bursts
- They're funny
- They ask fantastic questions
- They say what they think
- Their funny humour
- They're cheeky
- They're less bitchy than girls
- The rapport you can have
- Their excitement when they achieve
- They're lovable rogues
- They want to learn

What I like about teaching girls...

- Generally they're very motivated
- Usually they're able to complete tasks to expectation
- They keep everything clean and tidy (usually)
- They are better at staying on task
- They tend to follow through a task
- They're neat and tidy
- They want to please
- They're good at staying on task
- They're eager to learn
- They will sit and listen
- Their ability to concentrate
- Their ability to follow instructions and listen
- Their wish to please
- They always listen
- They sit and listen

- They're neat
- They're tidy
- They concentrate
- On the whole their behaviour is easier to manage
- They follow instructions
- They're more willing to listen
- They are able to help each other with ideas without digressing or just daydreaming
- Their calmness
- Their neatness
- Their presentation
- They're thorough
- They listen
- They plan and discuss
- They organize me!

What is striking every time is that the list for boys is invariably the most interesting, but how much do we tap into that enthusiasm, that fun and that energy? How often do we show boys that we appreciate their readiness to take risks and their honesty? And how often do we let them know that we value their weird and wonderful ideas that may take us off on a tangent, away from our agendas? Conversely, how often do we appear to be interested only in the things on the second list, and reward only those?

What I suggest to schools is that they write into their classroom observation and monitoring an examination of the ways in which they talk to boys and girls. It is a useful exercise to focus on the frequency, the quality and the nature of teacher interactions with boys and girls and to make that comparison. If the prospect sounds too daunting, capture one of your lessons on video – you could even watch it back with your class, explaining your purpose.

> I am the decisive element in the classroom. It is my personal approach that creates the climate. It is my daily mood that makes the weather. As a teacher I possess tremendous power to make a child's life miserable or joyous. I can be a tool of torture or an instrument of inspiration. I can humiliate or humour, hurt or heal. It is my response that decides whether a crisis will be escalated or de-escalated, a child humanized or dehumanized.
>
> *(Ginott 1972)*

In 2005, I delivered a day's training in a primary school in Tower Hamlets. As always, when talking about developing emotional intelligence, I stressed that it virtually goes without saying that it starts with ourselves. I urged the attendees to consider the quote from Ginott. 'On a bad day, it can really get to you,' I added. They smiled, even more knowingly than was the norm. Some time later, upon visiting the staff toilet, I discovered that they had this very same quote pinned to the back of all the cubicle doors.

One school in the National Education Breakthrough Programme in Raising Boys' Achievement decided to focus on teacher responses to boys' behaviour for a month, as an experiment. The Blessed Edward Oldthorne Catholic College in Warwickshire developed a whole-school approach to remove negative language from the school's classrooms and corridors using five specific approaches. Some were tried and tested techniques by people such as Bill Rogers and Andy Vass, while some were specifically created for the experiment. The results were quite staggering. The strategies were as follows:

- The broken record
- The passing technique
- Not saying please
- Agreement frames
- Reinforcing positive behaviour.

The broken record. The approach is just as it sounds. Instructions are repeated calmly and in exactly the same tone of voice until the required action takes place. (I heard one person suggest rather unkindly that the reason for this technique's success is that after so many repeated instructions boys run out of the language they need to talk their way out of doing something and end up just doing it for the sake of peace and quiet!)

The passing technique. This technique is useful for avoiding confrontation, but at the same time retaining power. For example, as he walks in late, you acknowledge the fact, but wave him to his seat, stating loudly and clearly so that everyone can hear 'OK, sit down, we'll sort this later.' It only works with the same individual in the same context for a limited number of times. Three maximum.

Not saying please. Removing the word 'please' from teachers' vocabulary, in the context of commands or requests, can have a very positive impact. 'Move over here, thank you', assumes that the action will take place, while using the word 'please' suggests that there is an element of choice to conform with the teacher's wishes or not.

Agreement frames. An agreement frame occurs when you say:

- what you can see to be true
- what you know to be true
- what you believe to be true
- what is compatible with what you are feeling.

Once this is established, it is possible to add bits that you would like people to agree to:

Thanks for getting here so promptly.

I imagine you're annoyed at having to miss part of your football practice.

In this way, there can be a discussion on his behaviour or attitude in a way that is completely non-confrontational.

Reinforcing positive behaviour. Boys need reminding of their social and learning responsibilities, but by the least confrontational means possible, not via constant and essentially negative means but via the reinforcement of positive behaviour: 'That's exactly what we're looking for, well done.'

Barrier 10

Emotional intelligence issues

Me?

Sing, me?
Dance?
Violin, me?
No chance

Act, me?
Paint?
Arty type?
I ain't

Write, me?
Poetry?
Like, me?
Not likely

Read, me?
Books?
Brain food?
Get stuffed

Think, me?
Think not

Care, me?
Go away
Scared, me?
NO WAY

Love, me?
Squeeze?
Hold me?

...please

Gary Wilson

Daniel Goleman, who has been credited by many as the person responsible for increasing public awareness of emotional intelligence, refers in his work to a clearly identifiable 'emotional gender gap'. In terms of developing emotional intelligence in boys, consider the following: when parents make up stories to tell their pre-school children, studies show that they use more 'emotion words' with their daughters than with their sons. It is also shown that when mothers talk to their daughters about feelings, they tend to discuss in more detail the emotional state itself than they do with their sons (except perhaps when discussing anger). Parents need to understand the importance of talking through feelings with boys and the importance of honouring their tender feelings. An American study by Carol Gilligan points to a significant difference between boys and girls in that boys take a pride in being lone, tough minded and autonomous, while girls really value connectedness. This continues for many into adulthood as Biddulph says in his book, *Manhood* (2004):

> People with friendship networks, intimacy, laughter and play in their lives have better immune systems, more energy, clearer thinking, are less prone to panic or extreme acts, and less likely to get sick or die. We are soothed and healed when we have a supporting net of social connections. Women usually have this but men do not.

He goes on to suggest that many adult males' lives are largely an act, since they often find themselves incapable of opening up and honestly expressing their feelings:

> Most men today don't have a life. What they have instead is an act. When a man is deeply unhappy, desperately worried, or utterly lonely or confused, he will often pretend the opposite, and so no one will know. Early in life little boys learn – from their parents, from school and from the big world outside – that they have to pretend. And most will do this for the rest of their lives.

If we wish to develop a more caring masculinity and turn out decent young men, work on emotional intelligence in schools is not a luxury, it is a necessity. Many of the strategies mentioned throughout this book contribute to this development.

Goleman's categorization of emotional intelligence, the SERIOUS model, is the most widely respected model.

Self-motivativation

Empathy

Reflection

Impulse control

Optimism

Understanding relationships

Self-awareness

Few would argue with the point that for many boys the development of *Self-motivation* is sadly lacking. Learned helplessness prior to even starting school, together with perceptions of the low intrinsic worth of schoolwork combined with a poor work ethic often encouraged by their peers, makes a fairly powerful recipe for extremely limited self-motivation. Some schools achieve success in the area of increasing boys' self-motivation by using some form of sport model such as the 'Three 'A's' model used by the SPACE (Sports Participation and Cultural Equality) project (www.space-project.co.uk). To achieve, they suggest, everyone has to have the three 'A's. Ambition and Aptitude, their model promotes, are worthless without Application. Certainly there are countless examples in sport of dedicated, highly motivated individuals who can serve as role models.

The extensive work of Baron Cohen has clearly identified women as by far the greatest empathizers. With regard to the need to develop *Empathy* in boys, there can be little doubt that this is an extremely significant area if we are to develop a caring masculinity. As an English teacher, I remember distinctly the experience of asking boys to write letters from the front during the First World War as part of Year 11's study of war poetry. It used to yield some wonderful examples of zero levels of empathy: 'Dear Mum, Having a lovely time ... home soon.' Many subject areas can be critical in aiding the development of empathy, not least English, drama and expressive arts.

The need for boys to develop their skills of *Reflection* is explored in great detail in a later section. In terms of all Goleman's categories of emotional intelligence, it could be argued that this is the most significant with regard to actively increasing the capacity of boys to learn. It is in this area of their learning process that many boys fall down.

The case for sustained work in the early years of schooling on developing *Impulse control* is perhaps best made by the famous 'Marshmallow Test' that psychologist Walter Mischel instigated in America in the 1960s. In the test, a group of four year olds were given a single marshmallow on a plate and told that that was theirs to eat. They were told that if they waited 15 minutes for the researcher to return from an 'errand', they could have a second one. Many ate the single marshmallow within seconds, while others put up with what seemed like an interminable wait to be rewarded with an extra one! The researcher followed the groups through adolescence to young adulthood. Those who had taken the marshmallow were socially less successful, stubborn, indecisive, overacted to irritations with sharp tempers and so on. As students, those who had acted patiently at four were more able to put their ideas into words, eager to learn and concentrate. The researchers were astonished to find that all those who deferred gratification achieved higher scores in all their tests.

> The basic belief that leads to Optimism is that setbacks or failures are due to circumstances that we can do something about to change them for the better.
>
> *(Goleman 1996)*

In schools, there is an overwhelming tendency for pupils to feel that mistakes are simply signs of failure, nothing more, nothing less. In business, mistakes are welcomed, often enthusiastically, as learning opportunities. We could significantly help create in our boys a far greater sense of *Optimism* if we were to engender this approach. Harry Levinson, pychoanalyst and business consultant, suggests that the art of being critical in a way that subsequently creates the basis of optimism contains four elements:

1   Be specific: don't just say this is a poor piece of work. Demoralization results if they do not know specifically what the problem is. Being specific about praise is just as important.

2   Offer a solution: without specific advice as to what can be done there is little room for optimism.

3   Be present: criticism and praise are most effective face to face. Boys respond far better to the genuine interest of their teacher than to something in writing.

4   Be sensitive: if we wish to develop empathy then we need to show it ourselves. Criticism without sensitivity creates openings for bitterness and resentment and little cause for anyone to feel that they have any worth or hope of improvement. (Adapted from Levinson 1992.)

The capacity for *Understanding relationships*, or the development of interpersonal intelligence, includes the ability to empathize with and connect with others. Those with particularly strong interpersonal skills will also be able to organize and lead groups as well as mediate between members of the group if there is conflict. On the surface, these would not appear to be the particular strengths of many boys (although it might be argued that the peer police are the exception that proves the rule!). Studying the skills of effective leaders and the characteristics of powerful mediators and peacemakers could provide a useful catalyst here. A strong focus on the development of interpersonal intelligence would be particularly well placed in PSHCE and drama.

With regard to developing *Self-awareness*, change is occurring in society at large in the early part of the twenty-first century. Many would suggest that there is a move towards developing a deeper self-awareness, with many men and women engaging in a personal journey within themselves. Self-enquiry materials abound from the work of Paul McKenna to the journey work for children created by Brandon Bays, which is enjoying some use in schools. How useful might it be to plant the seeds of this work within our schools, particularly for our young men?

Social and Emotional Aspects of Learning (SEAL) materials for primary schools (DfES 2005a) are loosely based upon Goleman's model, covering the following five domains:

- self-awareness
- managing feelings
- motivation
- empathy
- social skills.

As can be seen, the materials target the development of a range of skills that are particularly helpful to significant numbers of boys. These include the ability to deal with and resolve conflict effectively and fairly, manage strong feelings such as frustration, anger and anxiety as well as learning how to work and play co-operatively. At the time of writing, similar materials are about to be launched into high schools. But beware, they bear the legend 'Non-statutory, for guidance only' and it would appear that this is sometimes read as 'Place on top shelf in office and leave.' Again I would say these materials, particularly when built upon by a creative group of teachers, are more than extremely useful – they are vital.

Work on emotional intelligence in school has to begin with ourselves as teachers. It virtually goes without saying that establishing the right emotional classroom environment is a massively important prerequisite for learning.

The emotionally intelligent classroom

> It is a place where tears and other emotions are understood and allowed, where enthusiasm is inspired, where all questions are welcomed as a source of learning, where all feelings, values and opinions are significant and where a child or adult can be accepted for who they are.
>
> *(Corrie 2003)*

Negative emotions such as stress and anger preclude effective learning as significant amounts of research shows. This means that we cannot develop in our young men a sense of what it means to be emotionally intelligent if we have not created the environment in which we might nurture it and, most importantly, unless we model that caring role ourselves. 'All right you lot, come on shut up, we're doing emotional intelligence this afternoon!' is probably not the right approach! There are many ways of addressing the development of emotional intelligence and many useful classroom resources. Going one step further, Vital Connections, a team of holistic therapists and ex-teachers, have initiated a model for enhancing the development of emotional intelligence using a range of holistic approaches. For teachers to experience these techniques for themselves, it creates the added value of developing their emotional health and well-being, making them far more effective and focused in their teaching. In a society where more and more people are engaged in some form of personal journey to become more fulfilled and enlightened human beings, at peace with themselves, who are we to deny access to our young men for whom this work would be particularly beneficial?

Goleman's categorization of emotional intelligence	Vital Connections' route to developing emotional intelligence
Self-motivation	Do-in Japanese movement exercise
Empathy	Peer massage
Reflection	Meditation, quiet space, visualization
Impulse control	Yoga and chi kung
Optimism	Positive affirmations
Understanding relationships	Positive touch and the philosophy of yoga
Self-awareness	Breath work

Barrier 11

Mismatch of teaching styles to preferred ways of learning

Much is said about boys' preferred ways of working and the potential for a mismatch between that and teachers' preferred ways of teaching. Personally, I believe that there is a way that is basically just good practice, and as such it is good for all students. However, when done well, it hits all of the right buttons for boys, in key ways. First, it fulfils the need that many boys have – to know the big picture. Second, it reflects the need for appropriately activating the learner. Third, it encourages active demonstration of learning. Finally, it stresses the need to reflect on that learning. The model was developed by Alistair Smith (Smith et al 2003) and is known as the four stage accelerated learning cycle.

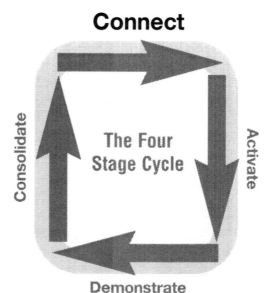

Connect

Consolidate

The Four Stage Cycle

Activate

Demonstrate

Connecting the learning

As far as most boys are concerned, they need to know exactly what the learning outcomes are going to be. To this end, it is helpful if the vast majority of teachers state these explicitly and clearly display them on the board to ensure that they remain constantly in view. Ideally, on either side of the board at the front of the room, ongoing work is displayed as a further visual way of making connections. Work that was done six months ago, or zappy posters, can sometimes have the opposite effect – disconnecting the learner. So how else can learning be connected? By using PowerPoints or an interactive whiteboard, presentations from the previous lesson can be scrolling through as the class file in or settle for the lesson. It may be that, as part of a reflective exercise in the previous lesson, pupils were asked to jot down on a sticky note anything that either stood out for them as something they would like to discuss further or something that they were stuck on and needed help with. If that is the case, then a review of the sticky notes is the place to start – to connect. More powerfully still, for many boys who are big picture thinkers, would be the use of maps. Concept mapping/idea mapping is an extremely boy-friendly tool because it helps boys to organize ideas, take notes effectively, remember and revise efficiently as well as enabling them to see the big picture. If, at the end of the previous lesson, be it science, geography or literacy, each pupil had to produce a simple map of what they learned, this would have significantly consolidated their learning. If the map was then shared with a partner so that each of them could add to each other's learning, even better. Bringing that map out at the beginning of the next lesson will powerfully re-connect the learning, particularly for the boy who needs to see where what he is going to do today fits in with the bigger scheme of things.

There are countless ways of connecting the learning and Alistair Smith would say that it is not just at the beginning of the lesson where this needs to happen. Indeed, he suggests that the best kind of lesson is like the television news: at the beginning there are the headlines about everything that is going to be covered; some way in there is a summary of what has been covered, together with the headlines of the bits are coming next; and so on until the final summary. In other words, constantly connecting, reviewing and reconnecting the learning.

Activating the learning

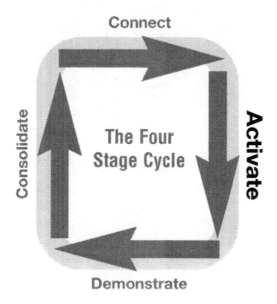

I heard of one teacher recently calling herself a 'Born again teacher'. I understand exactly what she means. Having spent practically 30 years teaching myself, I recall being told a tiny bit at the very beginning about how to teach, then for the remaining years I remember being told only WHAT I should teach. Now, suddenly in very recent times, we are actually talking about how children learn. And, what is more, it has become clear that it is never too early to start. You hear of infant and even nursery children describing themselves as being 'Tigger' learners or 'Owls' and so on (and Eeyores? 'Thank you for noticing me'). In schools in the Bristol area, there are posters on classroom walls describing the attributes of 'Curious Cat' learners or 'Creative Unicorn' learners. I heard of one seven year old who was asked to describe what learning was like and he replied it was like being on the motorway: 'Sometimes you're in the fast lane and everything's going well. Sometimes you're in the slow lane and people are overtaking you, but it's still OK, but then sometimes you have to come off onto the hard shoulder and somebody has to help you.' At this point, I am told, the whole class applauded him.

Talking about ourselves as learners and how we, as individuals, learn best is now well established in schools. In the context of boys' preferred learning styles, it does need some clarification. It may be that your discussion with pupils has gone as far as engaging them in a discussion about Gardner's multiple intelligences, maybe in the context of delivering assurances to someone who may not be 'word smart' that they may be 'body smart' or 'nature smart'. Again, as already stated, the discussion of learning preferences or strengths is something that can empower and engage pupils. However, I have seen this taken to extremes. An English department in a school in Alberta organized their classes according to their 'intelligence'. The young teacher that was teaching the 'linguistic' group was in her element. The young man who was teaching the 'bodily and kinesthetic' group was dead on his feet by lunchtime every day, looked 50 but was only in his twenties!

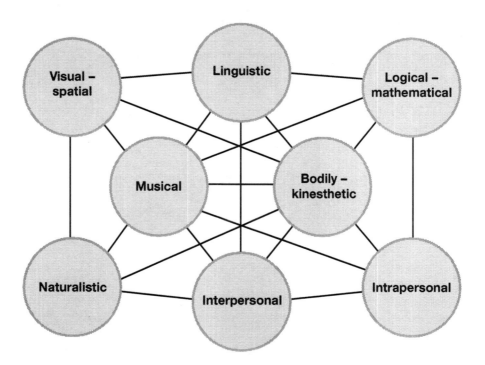

As far as VAK is concerned there is, or at least there should be, a giant health warning. It is not about identifying every pupil's learning style and teaching them everything in that way, relentlessly. Of course not, you say, who would be so foolish? Schools have been known to have youngsters write, and decorate, a huge V, A or K on the back of their planners for the teacher's benefit. The first part of the health warning is that we are talking about preferred learning styles here. In other words, we are talking about the pupil's strongest hand. The second part of the health warning is that the identification of preferred learning styles is not an exact science. Different measuring tools will often show different results. The third part we have to remember is that preferred learning styles are not fixed, they change over time and sometimes across subject areas.

It is undeniably true that, by whatever measure you choose, the vast majority of teachers, particularly primary teachers, tend to be visual learners. Sometimes, I have come across whole primary staffrooms full of visual learners. This goes against what is widely understood to be the national picture, across the general population, which suggests a fairly equal split but with kinesthetic learners being very slightly in the majority. What also appears to be the case is that we tend to teach in the way in which we, personally, learn best. For the kinesthetic learners there is clearly the potential for a mismatch in teaching and learning styles. Boys are not all kinesthetic learners, but, for at least a certain amount of their time in schools, many of the boys about whom this book concerns itself have a tendency towards preferring kinesthetic modes of learning. It is also true that these needs are insufficiently met. However, to teach boys who might have this preferred learning style in a kinesthetic way from morning until night would not only be totally exhausting, but it would also be wrong. Identify someone's strengths? Yes. Work to someone's strengths? Yes. Develop those areas of weakness, so they become well-rounded learners? Absolutely. The key message in the whole learning styles debate is that we need to teach in a balanced way, providing for all learners and increasing their range of ways of learning. Good primary schools have been highlighting in their planning for years where the opportunities exist in any given day for visual, auditory and kinesthetic learning to take place. Books such as *The Teacher's Toolkit* by Paul Ginnis provide a treasure trove of lessons that can be delivered in a visual, auditory and kinesthetic way.

What cannot be stressed enough, however, is the importance of talking about how we learn. I have often looked at preferred learning styles at parents' evenings. On these occasions, Year 6, Year 9 or Year 11 parents, together with their sons and teachers, begin, through discussion and then by using a reliable questionnaire, to explore their own preferred learning style. It is possible then to answer the question 'I don't get it, he's hopeless. I bought him a brand new desk for his revision and he hasn't sat at it once. Why is that?'. Should he be exhibiting a preference for kinesthetic learning (as would seem possible from the description), we can reply that the following ways might help.

box

Revision guide for kinesthetic learners

- Take frequent study breaks.
- Move around the room as you are revising.
- Try an exercise bike with your notes in front of you.
- Put the main points on cards and then sort in different ways.
- Skim through your notes first before looking at the detail.
- Create big maps or other graphic organizers, such as flow charts, of the areas of study.

It can also be useful to have simple home-made maps around the classroom, such as this one based on a map used by a school in the north of England which serves as a reminder of the discussions they had about preferred learning styles.

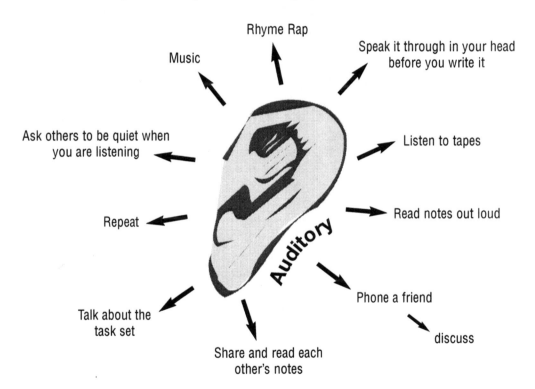

Meanwhile the following would help visual learners:

- use visual materials such as pictures, charts, maps and graphs
- use colour to highlight important points in text
- use colour coding for text
- use multimedia – for example, computers and videos
- study in a quiet place away from noise and disturbances
- use illustrated revision books
- visualize information
- watch TV documentaries around the subject
- make a big mind map of the area of work you have been studying.

Demonstrating the learning

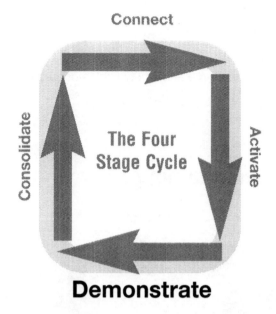

All too often we expect our pupils to demonstrate their learning by writing it down. Many boys will agree with me when I say that too much writing is done in schools. In Calgary, I have sat in on Gifted and Talented classes of 11 and 12 year olds for whole days, and there have been no pens or paper in evidence. Boredom? Disengagement? No. The only things that were flying around the room were ideas. The well-known and widely recognized model of how we learn best (see below) points out that simply being lectured at is by far the least effective way of learning. Reading is somewhat more effective. If, as teachers, we add audio-visual materials, some element of demonstration, and certainly discussion, then the learning tends to be significantly more powerful. It is interesting that the two most powerful ways of learning are practising something by doing and, above all, teaching others what we have just learned ourselves. Yet, with some exceptions (music, languages, PE), it could be argued that these are the two things that are done least in our classrooms. Furthermore, the potential within these two categories for a more kinesthetic approach is quite significant.

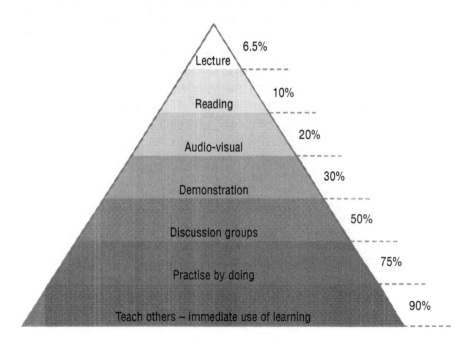

Read what these two old boys have to say:

The best way to learn is to teach.

(The Dalai Lama)

Tell me and I will forget. Show me and I may remember. Involve me, and I will understand.

(Confucius)

Consolidating the learning

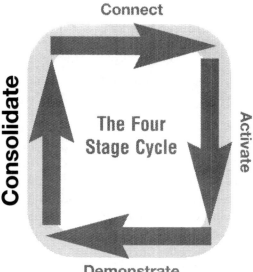

For boys, as I have said repeatedly, the most important parts of the lesson are those that allow them time to review and to reflect upon their learning. This is important for all pupils but boys in particular need, as an absolute minimum, the opportunity for a plenary at the end of the lesson. It is there to help them refer back to learning objectives and create a sense of completion and achievement. Furthermore, it prompts deeper thinking around what has been learned and how it has been learned. It should also be used to highlight where everything they have just explored fits in with the next stage of their learning. For the big picture thinker, therefore, consolidation at the end is vital. For many boys, whose main weakness in their learning process is their inability to reflect, this means of consolidation is an absolute necessity.

Barrier 12

Lack of opportunities for reflection

> Trying to learn without reviewing is like trying to fill the bath without putting the plug in.
>
> *(Mike Hughes)*

What is more, it can be argued, this is particularly the case as far as many boys are concerned. The 'Whoppinggreatbigbookofrecordsflicker' as described earlier are just the tip of the iceberg. Consider the gender gap in design technology subjects at GCSE level. Why is it as large as the gap in language based subjects? In a nutshell, it is because to many boys the hurdles that it presents are virtually the same because it is now a language-based subject in itself.

> Technology? Well, you spend ages planning and researching this damned silly thing you're gonna make [*and for him this still means cutting and pasting something from the internet, onto a blank Word document, sticking your name on it and handing it in*]. Then you make the damned silly thing [*usually the most successful part – apart from the finishing off bits sometimes – a lot of us never grow out of that part*]. Then afterwards you have to *think* about and, worst of all, *write* about how it went. You have to say 'If I'd only done this then that might have happened' or 'If I'd done that then it might have gone better'.
>
> *(15-year-old boy quoted in Hughes 2002)*

And, as we know, many boys have problems with premature evaluations!

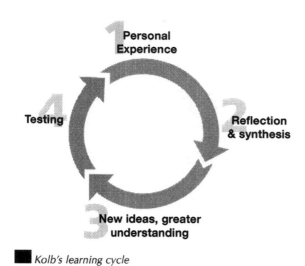

1 Personal Experience

2 Reflection & synthesis

3 New ideas, greater understanding

4 Testing

Kolb's learning cycle

It is many boys' inability to engage in the process of reflection that is one of the most significant barriers to their learning. Kolb's learning cycle clearly shows how significant reflection is to the learning process. Take out the element of reflection and boys are simply charging on to the next thing. So how do we help the 'Whoppinggreatbigbookofrecordflickers' and the 'premature evaluators' who run the real risk of turning into adult males who are incapable of dealing with complex emotions or even expressing their most basic feelings? Certainly choosing fiction over non-fiction is a useful beginning as described earlier, but perhaps the most significant school-based activity is the plenary. Yes, the plenary! Yet it is not uncommon for a staffroom to suddenly freeze at the mere mention of its name. 'Well, you see, colleagues, the plenary is the most important part of the lesson as far as the boy is concerned.' Silence. 'Well, actually,' comes the eventual reply, 'the plenary is that bit of the lesson we don't have time for because we have to fit this and this in, and from September we're going to have to squeeze this in as well.'

The bad news is that even just one plenary will not do. We need to go for *multi-plenaries*. Yes, it is true, a plenary is not just for Christmas. Young people, and particularly young boys, need the opportunity to reflect on their learning on a very regular basis – the very youngest probably every seven or eight minutes. Even high school students need rather more than one plenary and many are not even getting that. The irony is that prior to starting school, every child is a reflective learner: 'Why does the sea move dad? Why is the sky blue? Why? Why?' Recent research shows that by the end of a child's first term in Reception they are asking virtually no questions at all.

Why? For a start teachers have about 30 children in a class, so how can they possibly answer all of those questions. A fair amount of the time, teachers are also saying 'All right now children, settle down', and, as far as most of the children are concerned, there is an adult at the front of the room who knows absolutely everything, why should they question her. Added to this is the pressure felt by most teachers, usually imposed by outside agencies (Ofsted to be precise) to deliver at pace, and the opportunities for reflection effectively dwindle away almost before schooling has begun. Research shows quite clearly that as pupils pass through school, their main experience of questioning is barely adequate. The vast majority of questions that teachers ask, they answer themselves, and far too often question-and-answer sessions just activate the majority of girls, who tend to be fairly secure about their answers, and a few boys, whose flailing hands often indicate they are just 'having a go' – ask one of them and you may get a 'er … erm … I forgot!'. So how do we create meaningful opportunities for reflection?

In question-and-answer sessions it is possible to reduce boys' tendencies to engage their overactive risk-taking behaviour that encourages them to start waving as if they are drowning. The same method can be used to prevent the activation of the 'off' switch ('I don't do question-and-answer sessions'). At the teacher's request, everyone, with their partner, spends two or three minutes working out a number of answers to a question and the teacher then circulates around the room gathering responses.

Introduce opportunities, mid-session, for reflection. A proven technique is to engage pupils with partners in answering questions. Any combination of questions will do, and if they are displayed around the classroom, they also provide a constant reminder of the need to reflect on learning. Try the following time out/pit stop questions:

- What are the three most important things I have just learned? How can we now make sure that we remember them?
- Is there anything we're not clear about still?

Mini-plenaries in a range of learning styles can include: standing up, imagining that you are travelling on a crowded Tube and passing the time by talking to a neighbour about everything you have just learned. At a football match, it is half time, and standing to stretch your legs, you are discussing the highlights of the first 'half'.

Plenaries at the end of the session in a range of learning styles:

- Ask the pupils to produce a simple map of what they have learned and then swap ideas with a partner so that they can add to each other's maps.
- Each pupil writes down three things they have learned that lesson, they then share them with a partner, adding anything new to their own list. The pair then joins another pair, repeating the process, then the four joins with another four.
- At appropriate points in the lesson, pupils write questions based on what has been learned on pieces of paper. They are dropped into a box and at the end of the lesson they are drawn out by pupils in turn who have to answer them.
- Pupils generate a number of questions that would test their understanding of the lesson – then try some out on a partner.
- Ask pupils to write down as many words related to today's lesson as they can think of in one minute.
- Create a 'Blockbuster' game on the board, related to key learning points.
- At the beginning of the lesson, give one in three of the pupils a card containing a different question related to the lesson. During the course of the lesson they have to listen out for their question and at the end they have to explain it to the class. Use another third of the class the next time and so on.
- Do the hot potato exercise (see pages 72–73).
- Ask the class to answer the questions: 'What comes next lesson?' 'Where will this work take us now?'
- One pupil assumes the role of teacher and sums up the teaching points for the day, prompted if necessary by others.
- All pupils stand and the teacher nominates one to answer a (differentiated) question about the lesson. If wrong, the pupil sits down. If correct, the pupil nominates the next person to answer one of the teacher's questions.
- One pupil at a time is asked to take the hot seat and is required to answer questions as an expert learner.
- Use sets of cards with diagrams or images from the current topic. In pairs, one pupil has to describe what they see, while the other has to guess what has been described. (A third person can be used to ensure fair play.)
- Give an individual pupil a set amount of time to talk about some aspect of the learning. 'Stop the clock' from time to time to ask the views of others and enlist them to add to, or clarify, points.

- At given points in the lesson, pupils are asked to write appropriate questions that would test their understanding, on a strip of paper. The strips are collected in a box and, at the end, nominated pupils have to select a question and answer it.

- Set the pupils the task of 'beating the teacher' – with tough questions around the topic being studied.

- Ask the pupils to create a graphic representation of their learning, creating, for example, a flow chart, Venn diagram or fishbone diagram, depending upon the nature of the lesson.

- In pairs, pupils are asked to agree on three things they have learned that lesson, they then join another pair, hoping to add to their list. They then join four, and the four become eight, again adding to their lists.

- As a group, the main learning points are written down on sticky notes. One member of the group is responsible for collating, ordering or classifying the points, helped by their group.

- Pupils work in groups of four. The teacher shows one member of each group (for example, all the number ones) a map of the key learning points for the lesson. They then return to the group to help them re-create the map perfectly. Then all the number twos are sent for and so on. The first group to complete a carbon copy is the winner.

- Ask pupils to write on one sticky note 'The most important part of today's lesson was…' and on another 'One thing that I'd like to know more about is…'. Use the first notes to aid a whole-class review/plenary and the second to help connect the learning at the beginning of the next session.

- Provide cards with key learning points on that pupils have to sort in pairs.

> The only real object of education is to leave a man in the condition of continually asking questions.
>
> *(Tolstoy)*

 box

My favourite plenary

Used at a conference for Year 6 boys that I organized in Huddersfield in 2002. During the course of the day's workshops and presentations, there were, as you might expect, gaps for refreshments and so on. During the gaps the boys were allowed open access to a 'Big Brother Diary Room' that contained a young cameraman and several prompt cards on the wall. 'What did today mean to you?' 'What will you do differently in future because of today?' 'Do you have any messages for teachers or fellow pupils about how boys could do better?' At the end of the day, the whole conference watched (barely edited) highlights as a plenary.

 It's made me think that doing art can give you a future.

I thought the street dancers were cool – hope they do it at high school.

I want to write a rap with my friends all about how to get on at high school.

I'm going to ask if we can do a drama project with some older boys at the high school about bullying, like the one we saw.

It's made me think maybe I should be a peer befriender – it's not just for girls.

When I'm a dad, I'm going to make up stories for my children every night and tell them like Roop (Roop Singh, storyteller).

Barrier 13

Pupil grouping

It is my belief that setting is one of the most significant barriers to boys' achievement. No one wants to teach the bottom set Year 8 humanities group on Friday afternoon. Why? Because they are made up largely of disaffected boys who were told that they were not good enough either shortly after their arrival at high school or during that most critical of years when they are going to decide whether to opt for or against education – Year 8. As previously stated, we can persist in telling them that they are in a flexible situation, that they could move up, but how long will they believe in that – or themselves? Not long. In terms of how to make a difference to boys, I would say let us have a debate about pupil grouping. How much longer must education continue to be so arrogant as to think that young people learn only from adults, or that it is OK to put the linguistically most deprived in the linguistically most deprived environment? Yet, strangely, the debate that appears to be heard most in terms of pupil grouping in order to impact on raising boys' achievement is the one concerning single-sex education and, specifically, the one about teaching boys and girls in single-sex groups in comprehensive schools.

The Homerton report (Younger and Warrington 2005) dedicated a substantial amount of time to exploring the issues around single-sex grouping. In its preliminary research, it came up with a very mixed picture and then focused on three high schools in depth. One school during the research brought the experiment largely to a close as it found it unhelpful. The report itself concluded that it could work if it incorporated a range of prerequisites, including many elements of what could be argued to be just simply good practice that all pupils deserve: 'A proactive and assertive approach, avoiding the negative or confrontational' together with 'constant reinforcement of high expectations'. However, the report also clearly highlights potential hazards:

> Some questions remain, however, particularly a common worry about issues of classroom management and the extent to which all-boys' classes were more challenging for teachers. This was certainly the perception among some teachers in the three schools, and the concern that aggressively macho behaviour was exacerbated simply through a concentration of numbers, with a subsequent worsening of boys' behaviour.
>
> In some schools, boys'-only classes have become very challenging to teach, or stereotyping of expectation has established a macho regime which has alienated some boys.

Sadly, upon publication, the world, or at least the world's press, appeared to sense that it had been supplied with the answer it had been seeking.

Single-Sex Classes Needed to Help Boys Learn
Scotsman, UK, 28 May 2005

Single-sex classes backed by academics
Gulf Times, Qatar

Boys need separate classes
Hindustan Times, India

Academics support single-sex classes
Washington Times, DC

Study backs single-sex classes
New Zealand Herald, New Zealand

Single-sex classes boost boys' results!
Hindustan Times, India

Boys better in single-sex classes
Daily Times, Pakistan, 29 May 2005

As is the case with much of the world of education, everyone in it appears to be searching for THE reason why boys are underachieving. Having discovered the reason, then surely we can find THE answer. The QUICK FIX. We know there is no such thing as a simple cause for anything in the world of education (indeed, you are currently wading midway through the huge complexity of the issue), and we certainly know there is no quick fix.

Utilizing PASS statistical software, as a way of comprehensively measuring pupils' attitudes to a whole range of elements of their schooling, including their own attitudes to themselves as learners, one school discovered that girls' attitudes to school were rather more negative than boys. As an experiment, they began teaching them separately for core subjects. Illustrated overleaf are the changes in attitude over a term.

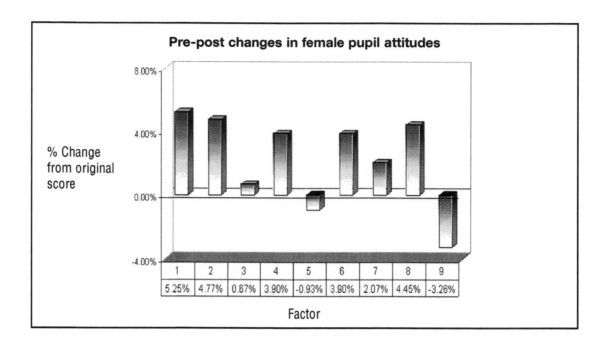

Quite good for the girls. The boys? The word 'plummet' springs to mind.

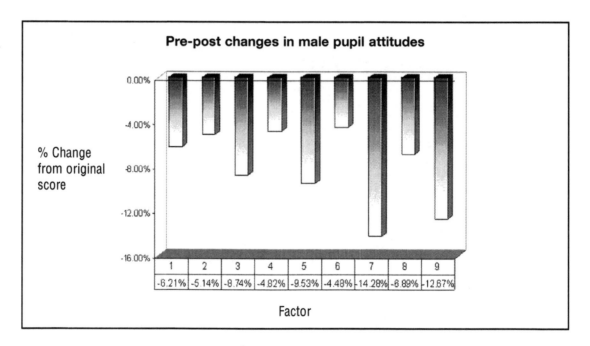

As far as the single-sex grouping issue is concerned, do we really want to start along a slippery slope that leads to a worsening of the so-called 'laddish culture' that is so despised? Following this path may significantly lessen the possibility of developing a more caring masculinity in our boys, something many of us have been toiling to produce for some considerable time now.

In terms of the far more significant debate on pupil grouping – the one on setting by ability and its impact on boys' underachievement – surely it can only be a matter of time before those reports that do exist in some number now, which indicate that setting does not benefit anyone other than possibly the parents, are superseded by reports that state that they are actually damaging, particularly to the boys we are concerned about.

Barrier 14

Inappropriate seating arrangements

It is not uncommon for schools to experiment with seating in ways that are intended to help boys. I have discovered many schools where they have seated their pupils boy/girl/boy/girl. Sometimes this has been applied in some subject areas and sometimes across the whole school. I believe that applying this system can not only be detrimental to girls' learning, but it can also run the risk of perpetuating the learned helplessness that is common in some boys. When in doubt, I always recommend asking the pupils themselves. I asked a group of Year 6 pupils, who had been seated boy/girl/boy/girl for some time, what they thought about the situation.

Most boys said they liked working with girls because:

- 'They're better at concentrating.'
- 'Because they help you.'
- 'Because they're brainier.'
- 'They do all the work.' (laughter) 'They tell you all the answers.' (more laughter)

The girls told me:

- 'Sometimes I don't like working with boys because they act stupid.'
- 'They don't go along with what you're doing, they just daydream.'
- 'And you don't know them as well. You want to get to them but they're too silly.'

I asked the girls why the boys said they like working with them.

- 'So we'll do all the work and they can just drift off.'
- 'So they can take all our ideas.'
- 'They make us do all the work, while they just relax.'

It is often very useful to agree a whole-school seating policy, as failure of the teacher to determine where pupils sit often creates difficulties. Many years ago at my own school I took the first step, sick of being called into the same classroom in September, January and May to be told that the problem was 'Those two boys at the back'. I began discussions as to how a seating policy could have a positive impact on learning. We all know where the disaffected or troublesome boys will sit given a free choice, usually at the back in the right-hand corner or along the sides just out of the peripheral vision of the teacher. The first step is the catch-all 'Teacher decides where you sit.' This is almost enough to represent a policy in itself. A whole range of valuable outcomes can clearly accrue as a result of what additional criteria you then apply and, crucially, how flexible you are in their application. If, for example, the aim in certain sessions is to provide maximum opportunity for reflection, it may be that from time to time you choose to promote boy/girl seating or that you establish a reflective partner system whereby you use any suitable partnership of pupils. It may be that in your seating plans language development is an issue, or avoidance of peer pressure. In either of these circumstances, you will know exactly where to sit pupils. Extremely significant, of course, is where pupils sit for group-work in order that the maximum benefit is gained. Again, flexibility is the key. It is not unheard of for schools to provide group lists for pupils to stick in the backs of their workbooks so that they can tick off the pupils they work with over the course of a term or school year, ensuring that sometimes they work with friends, sometimes with members of the opposite sex and sometimes with people they would never choose to work with.

 box

A whole-school seating policy

- The teacher decides where pupils sit.
- Criteria used should be made clear and be based on positive educational needs.
- Criteria should appreciate boys' needs to reflect on their work and avoid 'anti-boff', peer group pressures.
- Criteria should promote language development for bilingual pupils.
- Seating plan should be used directly to support group-work strategies; for example, by mixed gender, random or for larger groups.
- Flexibility should be promoted, with frequent changes in seating plans.

Barrier 15

Ineffective group-work

As we know, group-work is effective for boys when it engages, has clarity of purpose, has clear learning outcomes and is structured. Indeed, it can be extremely valuable for all concerned, not only in terms of exploring ideas but also in terms of developing social skills and self-esteem. When lacking structure and left to chance, boys may potentially either become overassertive or take on board the role of passenger, making no contribution whatsoever. In a huge number of primary schools and an increasing number of high schools where they are utilizing circle time, engaging boys in the activity is rarely problematic. Given the chance to share ideas and opinions and sense that they are being genuinely valued, boys respond very well. Circle time operates on the basis that everyone is actively listening. The co-operative nature of the activities employed are designed to develop personal and social skills and increase the sense in children that they are responsible for their own learning. The sense of trust and inclusion that is generated impacts profoundly on self-esteem. As such, this is engaging and positive group-work that is good for all and particularly good for those boys whose listening skills, interpersonal skills and low self-esteem are an issue.

Similar in some respects is another activity that is growing in popularity across the country. Philosophy for Children (P4C) creates 'Communities of Enquiry' when everyone is listened to and has the opportunity to express their views and feelings and be valued. In terms of activities that will help create more caring and thoughtful young men, I believe this is second to none.

> The aim of a thinking skills program such as P4C is not to turn children into philosophers or decision-makers, but to help them become more thoughtful, more reflective, more considerate and more reasonable individuals.
>
> *(Matthew Lipman 1990)*

P4C's ability to engage and motivate boys is, I believe, down to a variety of factors – not least its clear structure, its clarity of purpose and the sense that they are enjoying the genuine interest of other human beings. The fact that the enquiry takes them on a journey of exploration that they are creating as they go along, adds for many of them a spirit of adventure. The element of challenge – feeding into and maintaining the enquiry is a bonus, as is the perceived status of the mere term 'philosophy'. (I have come across several philosophy clubs around the country where boys are extremely active.) P4C has been around for many years and is used across the globe. It is based on extensive research and sits quite comfortably in a range of subjects from English to PSHCE, geography to RE. It can be used with Key Stage 1 pupils right through to adult groups.

One of the most straightforward P4C exercises typically includes groundwork on 'questioning', looking at the difference between a simple or shallow question and a deep or philosophical question. This is followed by the delivery of a piece of stimulus material in the shape of a picture, story, poem and so on. Pupils are then asked to think of a question that will take the group on an interesting journey philosophically. Next they are asked to share their question with a partner. After a few minutes they either choose which they consider between them to be the best question, or combine the two in some way. The teacher then writes the questions on the board, valuing each question individually and inviting the class to seek further clarification on the question from the questioner if necessary. Once written up, the 'best' question is voted for by the class. There are several ways of doing this, but with the questioners' eyes closed so that their friends will still speak to them if they chose not to vote for theirs! The enquiry then takes place. Using the following range of conventions, anyone can join in:

- I agree with you, because...
- I disagree with you, because...
- Can you explain what you mean exactly?
- I don't agree with any of you. What I think is...
- Meanwhile the teacher remains (in the words of Will Ord, chair of the Society for the Advancement of Philosophy in Education – www.sapere.net) the 'Guide on the side, not the sage on the stage!'

Using a picture of a large clothing advertising poster showing a young boy wearing a 'I'm lazy and proud of it' T-shirt as a stimulus to create a Community of Enquiry with a group of nine year olds, the following questions were elicited:

- Why has he chosen a T-shirt that says he's proud of being lazy?
- Is this boy interested in his life?
- *Is it clever not to work hard?*
- Where is he?
- How can he be proud if he's lazy?
- Does his T-shirt really describe his personality?
- What does it say on the back?

The one that they chose as the 'best' question is highlighted in italic. From the start of the exercise to the choice of question took about ten minutes. The enquiry lasted slightly longer. On the basis that the teacher and class were unknown to each other, the fact that together they got to the heart of the matter through a philosophical question is testimony to the strength of this process.

Other effective approaches to group-work include the following:

Hot potato
This group-work/thinking skills activity from Australia is popular with many. In groups of six, pupils are asked to choose the role that they wish to take in their group discussion. This is an interesting process in itself, so give them as long as it takes.

Writer	You write down the main points the group come up with.
Encourager	In a very friendly way, you make sure that everyone feels part of the work and everyone takes part.
Timer	You keep an eye on how the group is getting on and gently speed them up if anyone is wasting time.

Speaker   You will be asked to tell the rest of the class at the end what your group found out.

Manager   You are in charge, but you mustn't do it in a bossy way. You start things off and then ask others to take their turn.

Director   You make sure that people don't start going off the subject. Gently bring them back to the task by asking questions.

Then provide them with a simple map with a statement on it that covers a key learning point from the lesson or an area that you want to open up for exploration. With five groups of six, five statements will be needed. Allow the groups exactly two minutes to add their ideas to the simple maps and then pass them on for the next group to add their ideas. Repeat this process until all groups have had two minutes to add their ideas to the key statements. Allow time for feedback.

Round robin

After 'Hot potato', the children can then go on to this next stage. During this exercise the same rules apply as for 'Hot potato' but the statement for all groups is exactly the same. During the process, the challenge is significantly greater as each time a new map is presented, it becomes harder to add new, original ideas. In my view, it is particularly successful for boys because there is a real structure, a clear identification of roles, a real sense of purpose and a clear learning outcome. The time-limited, short-term goal element in conjunction with a hint of a challenge, also serve to make it an extremely boy-friendly activity.

Simply plenaries

Another ideal application for class or staff activity is to utilize a simple plenary at any point in the lesson, using the 'Round robin' approach. Why not go for a mini-plenary yourself now using the hot potato below?

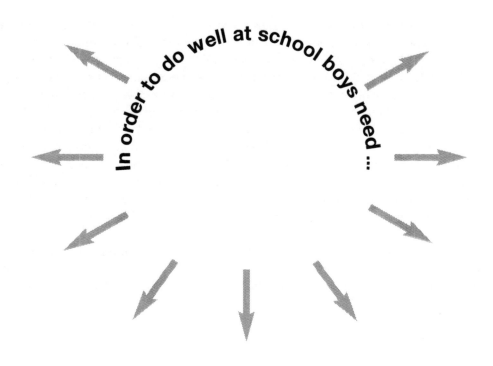

In order to do well at school boys need ...

Barrier 16

Peer pressure

Is it the caretaker, the secretary or a small group of boys in Year 5 or 6, or Years 10 and 11, who run your school? Indeed, in many schools it would appear to be the latter. The peer police are everywhere! They are the ones who determine how other boys should behave, whether it is appropriate to put your hand up in class, carry a school bag or do your homework. Even in the early years, the peer police cadets are already patrolling what is gender appropriate behaviour. By the time they are throwing their weight around at the top end of primary school or high school, they become a real force to be reckoned with, and probably one of the most significant barriers to boys' learning, which gives them permission to engage with any element of school.

In 2003, an Ofsted report on raising boys' achievement stated 'In *some* schools there are *some* boys who are stopping others from working.'

I was shocked! Shocked at the sheer inadequacy and apparent naivety of that statement. As everyone knows, peer pressure is endemic in our high schools and has been for some considerable time. The report should have said something like 'In many, many schools there are virtually whole cohorts of boys who are affected in some way by peer pressure, or the anti-swot culture as we know it. Indeed, every year countless numbers of boys fail to achieve what they clearly should have and their peers are often at least partly to blame. It is a crime against equal opportunities like any other and it has to be stamped out.' It should have said that, but it did not. The anti-swot/stew/spoff/boff/prof (depending upon where you live) culture is also evident in many, if not most, primary schools. Usually it appears in Year 6, often Year 5, but I have even come across it as early as Year 2. One teacher highlighted a small group of six-year-old boys who were members of a local 'crew', the oldest member of which was a 16 year old who represented the role model that everyone was duty bound to emulate.

In a class of 23 boys and five girls, I used a picture as the stimulus for a discussion in the form of a Philosophy for Children 'Community of Enquiry'. The picture showed a young girl sitting on the playground apparently injured and holding her leg. Two boys are in attendance bending over her.

The flavour of the discussion was that the two boys pictured had knocked the girl over and were in the process of covering up their crime, and persuading her that she should 'get up and pull herself together', so that they did not get into trouble. All the boys' contributions to the discussion were along this theme, except for the contribution from a boy called Dan. Somewhere in the middle of the pupil-led discussion, Dan suggested that the boys had come across the girl, injured on the floor, had seen that she was hurt and decided to help her. The discussion carried on apace, reverting to the previously agreed scenario. At the end I asked Dan to repeat his 'interesting contribution'. At this request he completely and absolutely changed his story, reverting to the group's agreed account.

Dan, it transpires, was THE peer leader in the class, and momentarily he had shown himself to be what many peer leaders are, a bright and sensitive young man. Given the opportunity to cover up his moment of 'weakness', that is exactly what he chose to do.

What is fascinating about many members of the peer police is that they can often be among the brightest boys in their year group, and, as Dan's story illustrates, often among the most sensitive. Their most obvious characteristic, however, is that they are invariably strong and natural-born leaders. I believe, therefore, that the main answer as to how we might significantly reduce the destructive power of the peer police is by transforming the peer police into a force for good. By this I mean utilizing their natural skills for leadership in a way that will have a positive impact on the life of the school, rather than the negative, often destructive impact they have at the moment.

Getting the peer police on board with a particular activity invariably means that automatically all boys will be granted a licence to participate. The peer police are exclusively responsible for handing out licences to other boys in a whole range of ways. Ensuring that they are engaged in any mentoring group, for example, means that it is fine for anyone to join. Using them to promote positive learning behaviour – for example, in posters showing them as readers or sports coaches – can send a powerful message to other boys, who are waiting for some sign of approval.

Giving them significant roles around the school can be another positive move. To be acceptable, these roles clearly need to have a certain amount of 'street cred'.

Every drama teacher knows that giving the role of victim to a renowned bully in a classroom improvization situation can be a powerful way of developing empathy and engaging with a potentially difficult issue head on. Many schools apply a similar principle in real life. Significant peer leaders are often engaged in work as peer mediators, peer befrienders or peer tutors. A scheme in the Central Foundation School in Islington, called the Anti Bullying Massive, is run by a group of predominantly boys who:

● trained in listening and advocacy skills
● identified potential hotspots for bullying
● developed an anti-bullying poster campaign
● patrol and do mediation work in the playground
● hold a lunchtime drop-in centre
● produced their own training video for others.

I firmly believe that the ultimate way to transform the peer police into a force for good has to be through the development of leadership programmes. These natural-born leaders need help to fine-tune their skills and utilize them to the full benefit not only of the school, but also for themselves. Subsequently, the community at large will be the ultimate beneficiaries as schools turn out more decent, self-respecting young men. To this end, such courses need to incorporate work on how they might:

- develop a sense of self-belief
- develop self-respect and respect in others
- use integrity
- inspire trust in others
- become positive examples
- develop empathy
- develop rapport
- develop the skills to organize others
- work not just as a team leader but also as a member of a team.

Such work is necessary if ultimately these boys are going to exert a positive influence over others.

Critical to the whole process is the first step: the development of a strong sense of self-belief (which will be explored later). Until they have refined that skill, boys cannot go on to instill it in others.

One of the greatest sadnesses is that it is on the boundaries of those areas of the curriculum, which are so critical in our task of creating a caring masculinity, that the peer police appear to patrol most vigorously.

At one of the boys' conferences that I organized in Kirklees, at which, as always, I was emphasizing the expressive, creative and performing arts, one guest was local book illustrator, Stephen Waterhouse. I was nervous about how he might go down, his presentation being immediately after lunch, during which 150 boys had all sampled a seven-item finger buffet and downed all of the e-numbers they could drink. Stephen, for his part, had stated that he did not need any fancy technological equipment, he was just going to 'show pictures and talk'. I thought, 'Well, that's it, disaster. Never mind, at least the morning had been a success.' Thankfully my fears for his session were totally ill-founded. The audience of boys and 20 headteachers were completely captivated by his account of life as an artist. He began by explaining how he had always loved art from being a small boy and that he 'stuck with it' and now he was a successful graphic artist. He showed posters of the millennium celebrations in London, paintings of the Golden Gate Bridge in San Francisco, Christmas cards, children's storybooks that he had written as well as illustrated and sketches that looked like Leonardo da Vinci cartoons. And then, the questions. They started slowly enough. One little voice piping up with the first, almost inevitable question, 'Which is your best picture?' Patiently, Stephen selected a favourite. Second question? 'Which is yer worst picture?' A smile from Stephen, followed by 'I don't think I've got a worst picture really.' The questions did improve. Then the final question from a young lad, hair all over the place, orange juice down his shirt, one sleeve rolled up, 'Where did you ... where did you get the courage?' Silence. Hardly a dry eye among the adults. What was he saying? 'How have you managed to stick with something as "soft" as art (it could have been music, or drama, poetry or dance) bearing in mind all the stick you're gonna get from your mates.' What was he saying about the powers of the peer police in determining not just how boys should behave, but also what kind of curriculum they should follow? What was the challenge the question presents to the education system? Bearing in mind how significant the affective subjects in the curriculum are in the battle to develop a more caring masculinity and turn out decent young men, the challenge to education is huge. How big a burden is it for a boy, turning up for the first day at the high school, carrying a violin case?

The man that draws the pictures in kids' books
Came to school today
Bit soft but
He were all right
He told us how he worked on his own all day
It wouldn't do for me
He were quite famous
He showed us some posters that he'd done
He sold them in London
Don't suppose he makes much
Then we were told to ask questions
I asked him which were his best picture
And he showed us
Then bloody Michael bloody Spencer
Asked him where he got the courage
I mean, what's all that about eh? Tosser
We got him after

Gary Wilson

A graduate teacher in his late twenties handed me a note after a training session, adding, 'Here you are, it was hard for me to write this down, because I've always really regretted what happened.'

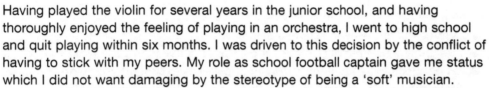

Having played the violin for several years in the junior school, and having thoroughly enjoyed the feeling of playing in an orchestra, I went to high school and quit playing within six months. I was driven to this decision by the conflict of having to stick with my peers. My role as school football captain gave me status which I did not want damaging by the stereotype of being a 'soft' musician.

Mike

 box

Primary assembly idea

Q: What words do we use to describe people who work hard? (In some cases I have heard nothing but positive words such as 'Superstar', 'Whizzkid' or 'Genius!' But it is, sad to say, extremely rarely.)

Teacher: What I always say is if someone is pointing the finger at you and calling you a swot, they are pointing three fingers back at themselves, saying 'I'm stupid me, I'm stupid me, I'm stupid me!'

Q: What's clever about not working hard?

You keep calling me swot
You call me prof
You keep calling me crawler
You call me boff
You keep calling me saddo
You call me geek
You keep calling me brainbox
You call me creep

One thing's clear, you're not so bright
YOU ... can't even get my name right

Gary Wilson

I believe that transforming our peer police into a force for good has to be the most powerful approach to the problem. But how else might we help to address the issue of peer pressure within our schools?

I believe this can be achieved by the following.

- Investigating the size of the problem by:
  - enlisting the school council in collecting individual testimonies
  - discussing the issue in PSHCE lessons
  - sharing staff's understanding of the scale of the problem at a staff meetings.

- Taking immediate practical steps such as:
  - addressing the issue in school assemblies
  - designing a number of sessions for PSHCE for all year groups
  - using specifically designed curriculum materials to support your work
  - normalizing the celebration of achievement via, for example, whole-year group achievement days
  - engaging peer leaders in responsible roles in the life of the school.

- Developing whole-school policy by:
  - engaging the school council to choose what they consider to be appropriate strategies; for example, zero tolerance on name calling, a whole-school acceptable language policy, a poster campaign, the introduction of peer befrienders or peer mediators
  - engaging peer leaders in developing policy.

- Presenting whole-school policy in:
  - assemblies
  - school planners
  - classroom poster form.

- Monitoring and reviewing effectiveness by:
  - engaging school council and peer leaders in the process.

Barrier 17

Inappropriate reward systems and lack of positive achievement culture

How appropriate is the reward system in your school? Does it maintain its currency for boys from Year 7 up to Year 11? Is it the case that by the end of Year 7 or 8, boys no longer see coming out to the front for stamps in their planners as a celebration of their success, but rather as public humiliation? Is it those peer police again who are determining to what extent boys can feel pride in their work and develop their self-worth as learners? It would appear to be something of a national characteristic that we are so poor at unconditionally accepting praise. If someone comments on our hair, then it is not uncommon to say 'Yes, but it needs washing.' If someone suggests that our little baby in the pram is beautiful, this is frequently followed by a hurried, 'Yes, but you should have heard her last night!' Add peer pressure into the mix and it becomes a potent weapon of confidence destruction.

Many primary teachers remark that boys begin school wanting nothing more than to please their teachers and end up wanting nothing more than to please their mates. One primary school I visited had, according to the head, no real issue with boys' underachievement. What they did have, however, was a problem with coasting boys who were putting in no real effort at all. We investigated the reward system together. It was evident that many boys perceived the reward system as being geared up to reward young children for turning up on time, sitting still and facing the right way. Why should the boys apply themselves in their work? What was in it for them?

Quite common in high schools is the scenario of boys eagerly accepting a public reward for achievements in sport, usually accompanied by a broad grin, firm handshake and even a wave to the mates. The same boy, on another occasion may be presented with an award for say, contributions to Year 10 poetry. For many, the hope would be that the ground opens up before they reach the stage. Indeed, many girls may feel the same way about public praise. But how do we know unless we ask them?

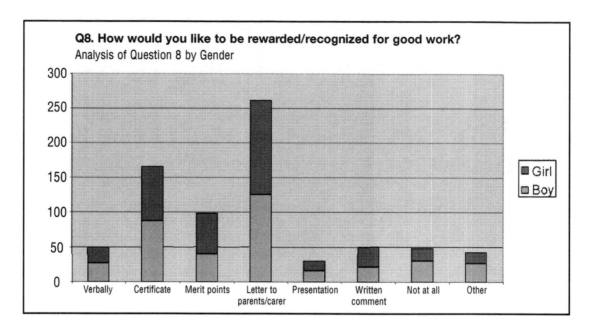

Sampling a school with an attitudinal questionnaire, specifically seeking responses to a range of ways in which rewards were considered acceptable, showed that by far the least preferred method of being given rewards was via a public presentation in assembly. The most popular method was a quiet letter (or postcard) home, or a certificate discreetly handed over. The message to that school? If you have not already started sending postcards and letters home, highlighting good work, then start. It is well understood that the biggest miscreant in the class will have the postcard from school stuck on the fridge at home until the day he retires. As far as many homes are concerned, it may be the only time they have ever received good news from their son's school. (These are particularly effective if they are posted to arrive on Saturday mornings, so that the whole family is around to celebrate.) The other message to the school? That will help but what are you going to do about developing a positive achievement culture within the school? It is not good enough to celebrate things quietly, out of the public eye; this could be seen as merely pandering to peer pressure. It is clearly vital to children's self-esteem, confidence and motivation that they all feel that it is good to achieve.

The graph below is from a school at the opposite end of the authority, a totally different school culture and totally different socio-economic grouping. The results are almost identical.

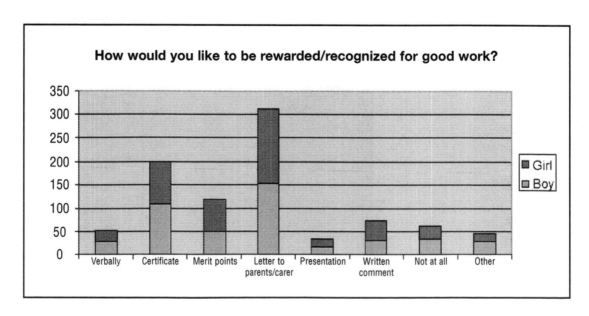

As previously stated, there is only one way to find out about how effective a reward system is, and that is to ask its beneficiaries. School councils are ideally placed to do that work; not only does it give them a chance to deal with a somewhat meatier agenda than many school councils but it also provides the opportunity to gauge views from Year 7 through to Year 11 or beyond. The following questions are a good place to start.

Is it cool:

- when a teacher writes a good comment on your work?
- when your work is put on display?
- when a teacher comments about your work in front of the rest of the class?
- when you get a merit or a credit?
- when the teacher asks you to read out your work?
- to receive an award in assembly?
- when you are asked to demonstrate or talk about something you know to others?
- when you get a letter or a postcard at home saying that you have done well?

NOW can you suggest one way in which you can improve the school's reward system?

The school council could even be given responsibility for designing the whole-school reward system and, as I have witnessed in one school, make a presentation to a staff meeting, outlining the new system. At this particular school, the final section of the presentation went something like, '…and now this is what we need *you* to do about it'.

Schools that have successfully introduced a wide range of reward systems to help them develop a positive achievement culture seem to have focused on many of the same key elements. Holding whole-school achievement days, for example, with each year group holding their own celebrations, is now quite commonplace. In this way public celebrations are smaller, the whole process is more normalized and everyone has more of a licence to succeed and celebrate success. Many schools follow up the celebration element with a focus on some very practical 'learning to learn' activities. In this way there is additional value added as the relationship between one achievement and the next is made very real.

A key element of success is also constantly reviewing the reward system on a two- or three-year basis. Reward systems rarely maintain their currency for too long. In the area of rewards, novelty certainly has an appeal. Postcards home, be they commercially produced, or home-grown, are a mainstay of many schools' reward systems.

I believe that it is important to constantly challenge ourselves to come up with fresh new ways of developing a positive achievement culture. To this end I recently promoted a texting scheme for sending messages to parents as part of Kirklees' LEA's 'Together We'll Succeed' campaign. Messages were sent out regularly regarding the importance of breakfasts, water, sleep and checking on the progress of revision timetables, together with information about local parents' support evenings and daily GCSE timetable reminders. The ultimate aim is to use the system at other times of the year to send good news home about achievements in school. More accessible than email and far more reliable and instant than pupil post!

Barrier 18

The laddish culture

 box

Hieroglyphic fragments from ancient Egypt bemoan the way contemporary youths were neglecting their studies and creating antisocial disturbances.

The model of masculinity presented by the boy culture of the school invariably mirrors the macho culture within the community local to the school. Moreover, the impact is far more potent if, as sometimes happens, it is actually condoned and therefore perpetuated by the school itself. If, for example, a high school's male PE department presents a tough male macho image, it can do a huge disservice to a substantial number of boys. For those boys who cannot live up to this model of masculinity, their confidence and self-esteem receive a constant battering. One such example was shared with me of a school with newly acquired sports college status where, on the first day that a new dance studio was opened, a small group of boys were trying out a few dance steps when the male head of PE appeared on the balcony and bellowed: 'Oi, you lads, what are you doing? Are you a load of wimps or what? Come on, clear off.' In total contrast, I know of another school where the male head of PE arranges all the school's theatre trips. The male PE teachers also make a point of praising boys for other achievements in informal chat in the changing room: 'Saw you playing trumpet in the school play the other night, you were brilliant.' They also have a zero tolerance on name calling of any kind, be it racist, sexist, homophobic, or 'swot', 'wimp', 'nerd' and so on, in the changing room, on the playing field and in the minibus.

> Sport is one of the primary sources of shaping a defective masculine image: arrogant, elitist, violent, unfeeling, individualistic, competitive and less than fully human.
>
> *(Peter West 1999)*
>
> School sport has to be adapted to suit the needs of children. It should be fun, inclusive, varied to suit all abilities, with only enough competition to create challenge. It should emphasize character, teamwork, pleasure of mastery and a sense of achieving personal best. *It is a huge part of boyhood, so we have to get it right.*
>
> *(Steve Biddulph 2003)*

I believe that it will be a struggle to have an impact on the way boys achieve unless we can impact on the way they are around the place. Not only that, but if we deal effectively with the boys in our class who demand most of the teacher's time and attention and behave in ways that are often antisocial and detrimental not only to their own learning but also to the learning of girls, then we are doing girls a huge service too. My own personal starting point at a school where I was senior manager was to enter into discussions with groups of not only boys, but also girls. The girls from whom I sought assistance in what I clearly indicated to them was a whole-school issue suggested very positive ways in which we might make boys behave more appropriately and subsequently improve their levels of achievement: 'I think boys would do better if they weren't always showing off in front of girls in lessons', 'It would be good if they behaved less immaturely', 'and stopped pestering us in the corridor'. It was as a result of such discussions that I determined that here was our starting point. It fitted the bill perfectly: it sought to have an impact on boys' behaviour in ways in which girls would also be the beneficiaries. We began by developing a sexual harassment policy. We engaged the school council, governors and non-teaching staff in its production and promoted it energetically via assemblies, parents' evenings and PSHCE lessons. Every classroom and every pupil planner contained a copy.

SEXUAL HARASSMENT

SEXUAL HARASSMENT	includes rude comments or 'joking', either spoken or written.
SEXUAL HARASSMENT	includes any unwelcomed touching.
SEXUAL HARASSMENT	includes the possession of pictures or books that may cause offence.

SEXUAL HARASSMENT IS WRONG

SEXUAL HARASSMENT	is unacceptable in society and where it occurs in school it will be taken very seriously and dealt with severely.

If you feel that you are a victim of, or a witness to, sexual harassment, then you must talk to *any* member of staff immediately. They'll know exactly what to do.

How else have schools had an impact on reducing the macho culture of the school? In more and more primary schools, particularly where their local communities present a tough macho culture that tries to seep in through the brickwork, through the windows and under the doors, alternative and imaginative approaches are being utilized. In one northern town in the heart of tough rugby league territory, I first came across children's yoga. This was a school's attempts to ameliorate the negative impact of the macho culture out on the streets. Chosen, in the first instance, because it was non-competitive and cross-cultural, the impact soon proved to be massively powerful in calming the whole school down. On one dull, grey, late autumn afternoon, I visited the school and saw five classes, one after another, bounce into the hall and each class, 20 minutes later, virtually float out again. During that 20 minutes they had laid down on their individual yoga mats, with their own class teacher participating too, while an experienced yoga teacher talked them very gently through their exercises as perfumed candles burned and peaceful music played. The use of yoga in this way is not just a solution for primary schools, it works very well with boys even at the higher end of the high school, who are amazed when working with groups such as Vital Connections from the northwest (www.vitalconnections.co.uk) to discover that football teams such as Wigan use yoga extensively in their training and that rugby star Jonny Wilkinson has a yoga routine that he practises before he steps out on to the field.

> To move forwards we need to look back to the eastern traditions of Tai Chi, Chi Kung, Yoga etc. It's apparent in today's society that there is a richness and wisdom in these traditions that has much to offer in helping us develop as a more caring, sharing, global civilization.
>
> *(Vital Connections)*

 box

Yoga exercises

Firebreath

Standing strong, with a sense that their feet are rooted into the earth and that a golden thread running from the top of their head is holding them upright, children draw in their first deep breath. (With practice children need to sense that their breath in, like a zipper, has to stretch from their toes to the tops of their heads, and their breath out has to go all the way from the top to the bottom.)

They now have to bring their awareness to their abdomen where they imagine that they are building a bright burning golden sun within. As it becomes brighter and brighter and warmer and warmer they are asked to imagine that their entire bodies are filling up with this golden sunlight. They are encouraged to feel the sunshine smile spread right through their bodies ending with a huge smile on their faces.

The true warrior

A preliminary discussion of what the term warrior means takes place, challenging common perceptions and exploring the full spectrum of meanings that can be attributed:

Strength with softness, wisdom with integrity and the ability to be a dependable leader and the calm within a storm.

The following process now takes place.

1 Alignment as before.
2 Legs apart to the point just before it becomes uncomfortable.
3 Raise arms on an inward breath, palms facing down and parallel to shoulders (feel strong and resilient, with the heart opened).
4 Turn right foot 90 degrees to the right and the left foot to the left.
5 Hips remain facing forwards.
6 As breath is released, the right knee is softened with the lower leg remaining at right angles to the ground.
7 The head turns to gaze at the right hand, focusing, warrior like on a specific target.
8 Repeat the process, facing left.

Peer massage is another activity which I actively promote in primary schools as another way of dampening down the laddish culture within a school, calming classrooms first thing in the morning or after a particularly 'boysterous' lunchtime. The basic routine involves pupils working in pairs, with one seated and another standing. The standing partner seeks permission from their friend to touch their back, and a well-practised routine begins, orchestrated by the teacher. Simple back and head massage techniques are utilized but are given child-friendly names and these are often incorporated into a storyline; for example, 'It's a gloriously sunny day and the big bright sun sends its golden rays in all directions ... suddenly the clouds begin to gather ... and then drops of rain begin to appear' and so on. The whole routine lasts three minutes or so and then the partners change places. Introduced into schools with young children, I have seen teachers teach the moves and then send them home for homework. As a result, parents have then built them into their children's bedtime routines. As far as boys are concerned, I believe the impact can be particularly powerful, often simply because it represents the kind of positive touch that many are starved of in their own lives. Someone planted an image in my mind once when discussing this work that I cannot shake free: 'Imagine how a pet dog or cat would be if it was never ever stroked.'

 box

The Massage in Schools Association (MISA)

Massage in Schools Association members, such as Vital Connections, train staff together with children in simple routines and cite the following as benefits:

- Children become calmer and have improved concentration.
- Children have more confidence and increased self-esteem.
- It teaches children to respect others and leads to social inclusion.
- There is a reduction in bullying and aggression.
- Emotional health improves.
- It helps children recognize good and bad touch.
- Children show improved motor skills.
- It encourages visual and kinesthetic learning.
- The teacher benefits from all these aspects.
- Massage is fun.

I believe peer massage to be a very powerful tool in so many ways, but as children pass through into high school there are many other types of massage techniques that can be utilized that might be considered more appropriate. Indian head massage, simple hand massage and so on are powerful ways of de-stressing and calming students down, not least, for example, in the run up to SATs and GCSEs. But above all, routines such as these are beginning to be widely used as ways of creating the right kind of emotional environment for learning.

Changing school cultures

Changing the culture of the corridor? Try mirrors on corridors or on staircases – children charge along, slow down to admire their reflection or adjust their hair or clothing, then carry on again, slower!

The creation of new social spaces, such as a sculpture lounge, can often be the source of big surprises. There are many boys who actually do not want to be charging around mindlessly, but would just like somewhere quiet to go for sanctuary.

One headteacher feels that he has significantly changed his school's culture and sense of purpose by having the school cleaned three times a day.

Tired of the ways boys charge around the corridors, giving each other fairly hefty whacks on the shoulder as a way of greeting each other, I wrote the poem opposite specifically to use in school assembly. This was just one of a half-termly series of assemblies designed to explore the laddish culture in school in such a way that it would be memorable. Together with a guitar-accompanied rendition of the Beatles' 'Nowhere Man', my performance of the following opus was intended as a way of encouraging the school to consider just how boys were 'around the place'.

Nowhere Boys
(Read at pace, in the style of a punk poet)

Rampaging round the corridors,
Making loadsa noise,
If anybody asks us we're the going nowhere boys.

'What you up to, where you going?'
that's what they want to know
we're going nowhere fast, we don't do nothing slow.

Rampaging round the corridors,
Making loadsa noise,
If anybody asks us we're the going nowhere boys.

If there's a fight we'll sniff it out
And give it our support,
Cheer and sneer then disappear, before we get caught.

Rampaging round the corridors,
Making loadsa noise,
If anybody asks us we're the going nowhere boys.

'What you up to, where you been?'
S'what they all want to know
We don't stop to answer them, always on the go.

Rampaging round the corridors,
Making loadsa noise,
If anybody asks us we're the going nowhere boys.

When we get in classrooms,
Sometimes it's nice to sit
Makes a change from charging round, resting for a bit.

(slow the pace right down)

Me, I'm thinking about break,
Feed my face, have a laugh,
I just can't be doing with this geography and maths.

Rampaging round my brain cells
It's just a load of noise
If anybody asks us we're the going nowhere boys.

Teacher just said something
Don't know what he said,
My mate put his hand up! Right, after this he's dead.

Rampaging round the corridors,
Making loadsa noise,
If anybody asks us we're the going nowhere boys.

Gary Wilson

It always provokes a response, not least the penultimate verse which is not about the culture of the corridor, but instead about the phenomena that I refer to as the 'anti-swot culture' or 'anti-boff' as it is in many parts of the country ('anti-stew' in Belfast and 'anti-spoff' in Scotland!). Indeed, wherever you travel in the UK, there are lots of words, predominantly used in high schools, for people who work hard. And none of them are complimentary. Sometimes, I use this poem in primary school assemblies when I talk about the onset of peer pressure. It is interesting that in some primary schools when I start off the assembly by asking what words we use to describe people who work hard, sometimes I get answers such as 'Superstar' and 'Whizz Kid'. But those schools are rare. What has happened occasionally, however, is that a few days later I receive a poem like this one:

The Going Somewhere Boys (an extract)

Rampaging round the corridors
Making loadsa noise
If anybody asks us we're the going SOMEWHERE boys.

We're going to the library
Selecting lots of books
We're also doing tidying up
To improve how it looks.

We're going to Befrienders
To help and give advice
To solve children's problems
And help them to feel nice.

We're going back to the classroom,
We like to be on time
We need to get our brains in gear
We've a mountain to climb!

Class 5C Chickenley Junior Infant and Nursery

Another assembly involved eggs – raw eggs. Inspired by successful experiments in the USA with bags of flour and sugar, I decided to give my own Year 9 form the responsibility of caring for an egg all day. It was a minor success, despite several drawbacks. I am pretty sure now, in retrospect, it might have been sensible to mention to other staff in the school what I was up to and what I had in mind. And, of course, there was the small matter of a few damaged geography textbooks.

In a nutshell (eggshell?), I instructed my form to all bring in an egg from home. All the girls remembered, only three of the boys did. I had covered all eventualities and brought in 18 from my own hens at home. Two boys broke theirs getting them out of the box (the first time they had ever attempted this task, I believe). They received replacements. The task was then very simple: they had to ensure that they returned their eggs intact at the end of the day. One boy returned to the form room within minutes of the end of registration: 'Sir I was throwing it up and down in the air and then I dropped it. Then I stomped on it.' I was not quite sure why the final part of this act of destruction was necessary but I was suitably unsympathetic. Another boy reported a small group of his friends attempting to lock their eggs in their lockers until the end of the day.

At break time, one boy was holding out his egg in the palm of his hand and proudly announcing to all who cared to listen that he still had his. 'Splat'. Jealousy is a terrible thing. Another became quite attached to his egg after he had drawn a very striking likeness to the then headteacher on his, but sadly it did not make it past lunchtime.

At the end of the day I waited expectantly for eggs to be returned. The three boys who returned them intact at the end of the day were precisely those whom I would have predicted capable of such a test. All but three girls returned the eggs. The three whose eggs had smashed had all been victims of boys' attacks.

And the assembly? Again, all about the way boys are around the place, about remembering homework(!) and about how, given just a little responsibility to care and look after something, most girls could manage that very well, but many, indeed most, boys could not. A little basic perhaps, but another assembly that many remembered for some time.

The influence of street culture

Boys, particularly at the point of transition from primary school to high school, need all the help that they can get in terms of developing an identity for themselves that sits comfortably not only with them, but also with their peers. If elements of their own culture are not valued, or at the very least acknowledged, then they look elsewhere to find that connection. Currently, for many, that somewhere else is the street. Street culture is not all bad and where schools have incorporated elements of street art, for example, it has introduced a new vigour into art lessons as well as, most importantly, given boys a greater sense of engagement with the school. Almondbury High School, aware of the very strong pull of the local 'shop front' culture, elected to give a very strong and very public acknowledgement of the positive, expressive arts elements. Engaging with a local street artist a group of disaffected boys produced a huge piece of graffiti art which subsequently was hung in a town centre location. Public interest led ultimately to the group being commissioned to produce other pieces of community art including the decoration of a local basketball court. Boys' interest in extra-curricular music was multiplied hundredfold with the introduction of lunchtime recording sessions at which boys produced, in remarkable turnaround time, CDs of their self-penned raps. A local street dance crew got boys interested in dance for the first time. Far from being a culture that is to be shied away from or ignored, the vibrancy of many of its elements can help to powerfully engage boys and lead them to see their educational experience as far more real.

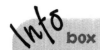 **box**

Pause for thought

A business model might be an appropriate one to apply here. Imagine that 'street culture' is a rival firm that has opened up for business down the street and it is taking away all your customers. What are you going to do?

First consider what it is offering to your customers that you are not providing, could it be:

- protection
- friendship
- support
- identity
- a close-knit community?

What is this telling you?

Barrier 20

Mismatch between assessment/examination methods and preferred ways of working

Where high schools are achieving greater levels of success with significant numbers of boys, they are focusing very clearly on the issue of boys' preferred ways of working. Traditionally, coursework, say in geography, for example, has been set in October, to be handed in by February. When do significant numbers of boys start this? Hands up. 'February' you say. 'Good school' I say. Many say 'March'. Where schools are having success, they are saying to their boys – here is the first chapter, here are the criteria you have to meet and it has to be in at the end of October. The teachers then turn the work around quickly, adding useful and supportive feedback, usually in conjunction with verbal feedback – then on to the next chapter. Boy-friendly chunks. For many boys it has to be short-term goals coupled with short-term gratification.

Boy-friendly
CHUNKS

One school in the north of England chose to adopt only three major strategies to raise boys' achievement. First, they ensured that clarity of learning outcomes was a top priority in all classrooms. Second, they ensured that all teachers were allowing time for a quality plenary session. Senior managers spent a whole term visiting classrooms at the beginning or end of lessons to monitor and support this move. Third, they insisted that all departments approached coursework in short sections.

It is well documented that examinations suit most boys' tendency towards risk-taking behaviour and that the often wordier and invariably more protracted nature of coursework does not serve boys as well as it does many girls. For many boys, having to spend time in preparation, research and evaluation can seriously impact negatively on their engagement with the process until adequate supporting strategies are applied.

Barrier 21

Lack of positive male role models

The shortage of positive male role models in young boys' lives is well understood. Within those areas that are perhaps the most significant to the majority – sport and the media – behaviour and attitude are often significantly less than positive. Boys need loving, caring men in their lives to balance the distorted and negative image of men in the media. What is problematic is what do we do about it?

Starting with the home, before boys even begin school, the message that needs to be clearly communicated is the significant part the father or the mother's male partner, older brother or any male member of the extended family can play. If it is mum who models all the positive learning behaviours, reads to the boy before he starts school and is the only one who attends parent support evenings or offers to work in school, then this represents a missed opportunity on a grand scale. Older males who are also in learning, be it as older school pupils, college students or apprentices, should be presenting themselves as positive role models as co-learners. Magazines and other publications, often from the most respectable of sources, purporting to be about the role of parents in their child's education, frequently stereotype the role of fathers or omit to mention that they have a role at all. We must not make that mistake in our displays or our home–school communications. Older males in the family also need reminding of the powerful role they play in developing a boy's self-esteem and confidence. Anyone who has witnessed parents as spectators at Sunday morning football will probably have winced at the comments of many dads, who, in the heat of the moment are frequently to be heard baying for blood or at least screaming at their boys, urging them on to 'Take him out!' or 'Get in there!'.

Forty-eight per cent of boys have no experience of a male teacher at all until they reach the high school, and this figure is rapidly increasing. There is a lot to be said for the point that it is the quality of the teacher, male or female, which is the most critical factor. Indeed, there is research evidence that shows that the gender of the teacher goes either unnoticed or the lack of male teachers is considered irrelevant by some pupils. For some boys, the total lack of adult male role models in the first seven years of school can be a huge issue, and it is one that is set to grow worse. Of course, it can be argued, this is an issue for girls too.

The reasons behind such under-representation of males in the early years of teaching are well understood. For many, the concerns about accusations of inappropriate behaviour are keeping them away. The fact that to their own peers, they might be perceived as engaging in an 'unmanly' activity can also dissuade many from working with younger children. Working with older children, however, does not carry the same stigma as, sadly, the myth that each ascending year of education carries more prestige is one that continues to perpetuate.

The reasons that some parents repeatedly give for wanting more male teachers in primary schools are not particularly helpful. Men that might 'keep the boys in order' and 'do' the football are not exactly what we are looking for. For pupils, boys in particular, male teachers are liked when they are fun, know what they are doing, set appropriate parameters and are fair in their dealings with children. More importantly, in terms of male teachers providing boys with positive male role models, it is not just any men that we need but the kind of men who present a caring masculinity.

> Not knowing the inner world of real men, each boy is forced to base his idea of self on a thinly drawn image gleaned from television, cinema and his peers, which he then acts out, hoping to prove he is a man.
>
> *(Biddulph 2004)*

Older societies and, indeed, even our own in the past have provided adult mentors from outside the immediate family to guide boys through adolescence. As a society, we are presenting less and less of this type of support to young adolescent males as time goes on. Youth groups and old-style apprenticeships are steadily dwindling away. As boys grow, the only opportunities that seem to remain for male mentoring appear to be in the field of sport, and if that is typically shrouded in a tough, macho culture, it leaves many boys still wanting.

> A boy needs help to learn about his own gifts and identity, and help to learn how to identify someone who has mastered the skills that are the birthright of his nature. Their lives seldom expose them to mature men doing things of such quality as to inspire a boy's emulation and his willingness to discipline himself in anticipation of being ready for his own chance later in life. In this light we should not be surprised that our teenagers have grown apathetic about preparing for roles that are invisible to them or that exercise no charm over their imaginations.
>
> *(John Palmour in Harding 1992)*

The choice of male mentors from outside school would be those who have a very clear sense of purpose, who are becoming fulfilled in their own lives and therefore are well placed to inspire in boys the ultimate search for their own sense of purpose. To this end, many schools now effectively link with higher and further education institutions to find male mentors for individuals or groups of boys. Past students who have achieved in business locally are of particular value as they exhibit to boys a very real connection between their current circumstance and the potential for success in their wider community. Local sportsmen are also used effectively in a variety of circumstances, but chosen with care to ensure that they present a positive male role model. The creative possibilities of such schemes is typified by the award-winning Boys2men project, a mentoring scheme that works with disaffected inner-city black boys in London. Part of the scheme includes engaging the boys in nurturing others in return for their own support. The boys regularly visit old people's homes to talk and serve food.

Given the limited availability of such opportunities, there is ample evidence to show that school-based mentoring can make a contribution to the need of boys for support outside the family, particularly at a time, during adolescence, when many boys and their fathers temporarily tend to drift apart. The role can be performed by either male or female teachers, but I believe that it would not be inappropriate to make an informed choice based upon home circumstances. As we know, many young men have no adult male at home whatsoever.

Mentoring schemes that are effective in schools tend to be those where members of staff are at once supportive and also proactive on behalf of their mentees. The Homerton report (Younger and Warrington 2005) on raising boys' achievement highlights what children have to say about good mentoring. According to them, good mentors:

- don't show irritation and have lots of patience
- are willing to listen to students and are enthusiastic for them
- enable students to establish a dialogue with them
- convince students of their own ability and what they can achieve
- are prepared to accept that a student is not perfect, and to look ahead and take a positive view on things, rather than simply 'going on and on if you've taken a dip'
- are straight talking, honest and genuine: 'he's dead canny and gets on so well with us'
- 'give you advice and support, and strategies to help you learn, but give you responsibility because you have to go and do it, to take responsibility yourself for your time-management, and your own revision'
- realize there is life outside school!

Such schemes are clearly invaluable, but as many schools know to their cost, they can be extremely resource intensive. For my part, for several years I mentored Year 8 boys in that they had a structured and effective programme.

 box

Year 8 mentoring programme tool

The solution-focused approach to building aspirations: 'Rolling the carpet out a little at a time'

Using a pre-prepared sticker that says, for example, 'This is how well I'm doing at school' or 'This is what my teacher thinks of me' or 'This is how caring I am as a person', the mentee places the sticker where they feel it best fits their current situation on a line of 0–10. Placing it at, say, 5 or 6 may be initially demoralizing. However, the next part of the exercise is designed to make them feel good about themselves despite this lowly position. Ask the mentee to write down, in the space from zero to wherever they placed the sticker, all the reasons why it is not at zero. THEN in the space below the next number, write down just one or two things they need to do to move onto that number and NOT to 10.

School teams and clubs within schools that attract boys should be viewed as further opportunities for mentoring in the sense that the leaders and coaches are providing further models for boys to learn from. With this very much in mind, those responsible for leadership roles need to exercise great care in the model that they present to boys. Where schools have close links with local teams and clubs, I believe that some measure of responsibility lies with the school to ensure that the nature of the coaching is in line with what is delivered in school. In turn, coaches themselves have a significant responsibility to deal with aggressive behaviour both on and off the pitch.

Any adult males in the lives of young boys should be aware of the often extremely fragile nature of many young boys' developing identity. Dealing with boys in ways that they recognize to be fun, genuinely warm, fair but not 'soft', firm but not tough, will guarantee success.

Often overlooked is the role that older pupils can play in terms of providing boys with positive male role models. Teachers in one of the country's leading boys' independent schools, where the issues were around peer pressure and emotional intelligence, declared themselves to be delighted that the head boy for the current academic year was not only outstanding academically and outstanding at sport, but he was also a brilliant, multi-award winning singer. The first two of course worked well for him as they do for many boys – giving him a licence to achieve because he could also be 'one of the lads'. The third, his ability as a singer, meant that school music in general, and singing in particular, had received a tremendous boost that year. 'We don't want him to leave at the end of the year!' one teacher said. 'Don't let him then!' I replied. I wasn't suggesting incarceration but maintaining an attachment with the boy for the sake of other boys in the school, for at least as long as he remained in the memory of their current Year 7. Such pupils are priceless and should be cherished.

There are many ways in which boys can be used as positive male role models for younger boys. Fairly common is the practice of attaching older boys to younger boys (Year 11 to Year 7 for example) as an additional element of a school's pastoral system. Vertical tutor grouping in high schools, where forms are made up of a small group of pupils from each of Years 7, 8, 9, 10 and 11, similarly offers the opportunity to provide younger boys (and girls too) with additional pastoral support. This method is often adopted as a means of reducing bullying and peer pressure. House systems are experiencing a recent resurgence in schools from every phase, again with the intention of complementing the pastoral system and adding a competitive element to academic and sporting achievement.

Boys working as peer tutors in a range of ways not only impact upon their younger partners or the less able, but also on their own self-esteem.

 box

Shared reading

This process whereby older boys with low self-esteem, but with adequate reading skills, are used to teach younger boys with lesser reading skills is a case in point. Training is first given to the tutors and significant public status is afforded to them and their successful students.

In displays, older boys (as discussed earlier) can be very effectively used around the school to promote positive learning behaviour. The use of scale is extremely significant, and the more professional in appearance, the more powerful the impact.

Where such a display can be used to highlight an occasion where you have 'caught someone doing well', the impact on the individual can also be considerable.

Much good can come from placing displays of work produced by high school boys in primary schools. For current primary school boys to be able to see the kind of work that they will be able to do when they get to the high school, as actually produced by someone they know, can be extremely beneficial. High school boys could and should be used far more frequently as positive role models for their counterparts in feeder primary schools, not just because they are known quantities, but also because it encourages, in a meaningful way, a 'bigger picture' view of education. Older boys could be writing for younger boys, working as junior playleaders or coaches, carrying out their work experience in primary school or volunteering their services after school. Many primary schools are just crying out for positive male role models, and high schools can really help.

box

Older boys operating as positive male role models

- junior play leaders
- peer befrienders
- peer tutors (such as shared reading)
- peer mediators (the Anti-Bullying Missive)
- on work experience at feeder primaries
- as peer support (Year 11 adopting Year 7 forms)
- as school councillors
- as librarians.

Being a buddy

When I first became a form buddy I had to show a group of Year 6s around the school. When the Year 6s became Year 7s I was expected to help out at form period in any way the teacher felt fit. Sometimes this involved reading the notices or helping with some homework; this helps you give someone a head start at Colne Valley. I feel that this is a good thing which is worth doing, particularly when a Year 7 stops you on the corridor and you can help them. This has given me a real sense of pride.

Martyn, Year 11

Being a form rep

The role of the form rep is to put forward the views and problems of your form. Being a form rep allows you to help organize fund-raising events and trips for your year group. It also allows you to help run the school from a pupil's point of view.

Hal, Year 9

Boys working as peer befrienders (or similar schemes) not only play a useful role in the life of the school, but they also present themselves as positive male role models, displaying a caring masculinity, to others. Offering peer befriending as a scheme in schools, it is clearly important to ensure participation by girls AND boys. Typically, in primary schools over the years where I have seen such schemes in operation, there is often a framed photograph in the school's entrance hall with 15 girls proudly displaying their enamel 'Befrienders' badge. Meanwhile, two boys can be seen desperately trying to hide behind them on the photograph, because that is not what boys do – talk and listen and care!

box

Peer befrienders

- Young people who are trained as peer helpers share experiences and feelings of being bullied for a whole range of reasons, including the fact that they work hard.
- They offer help to their peers in areas that include bullying, friendship difficulties and settling into a new school.
- Volunteers have regular meetings with adult co-ordinators to ensure that help is available when necessary.
- The volunteers themselves gain increased self-esteem, confidence, friendship skills, improved communication skills, perspective-taking skills, citizenship and leadership skills from direct involvement in running the scheme and actively helping others.
- They begin to understand the effect that bullying and other forms of antisocial behaviour have on others by listening to children's experiences of being bullied and how this has affected them.
- This increase in awareness leads to changes in attitude and behaviour, with an increased capacity for pro-social behaviour.
- Their growing self-esteem and confidence comes from recognizing that they can make a difference by helping others.

Barrier 22

The use of non-performance enhancing drugs

The extensive use among boys of cannabis clearly impacts negatively upon their performance in school, in several ways. Primarily there are the immediate effects of smoking cannabis that create the antithesis of preparedness for learning. Alertness, energy and focus are not in the equation at all. The health risks, depending on where you read about them, range from 'significant' to 'a psychotic nightmare waiting to happen'. It is clear that the cannabis being smoked now is many, many times stronger than that which was smoked in the 1960s. The THC content (the potent element of the drug) is around 40 times greater. Then there is the potential draw (no pun intended) of the lifestyle of drug dealers – that in itself represents for some an attractive alternative to working hard in school in order to reap rich rewards in the employment market. I have heard, on many occasions, 11 and 12 year olds talk about their older brothers who have fancy cars, cool clothes, phones, girlfriends and lots of money as a result of selling drugs on the street. Several have expressed concerns not only about their safety, but also about how it is tempting many of their own friends to follow that path. One told me, 'I think it's bad that we don't have a stronger drugs education – you know the kind where they tell you all the dangers and that, because some people think it's easy and it's safe and that's not right.'

 If 12 year olds are expressing concern about the lack of effectiveness of drugs education in schools, perhaps it is time we examined it more closely. The concern is that there are schools that could do more both about the education side of the issue and about stamping it out. Admittedly, it does not help when you hear from some high authority that there is no drug problem in your white, leafy lane, middle-class area. Why is this so? Because there is no crime attached to it – everyone has money and they can afford to buy it! One local authority, in a confidential report that involved interviewing all 1,100 pupils in one school, cited the fact that upwards of 80 pupils in the school could be relied upon on any given day to supply anyone with cannabis. Similar figures were reported in schools with comparable socio-economic backgrounds. It can be precisely these schools where there is a flat denial of any such activity, fearful as they are of being tainted with any suggestion that they have a drug problem.

The part that cannabis plays in boys' lives is an interesting area to explore. Peer pressure, as might be expected, raises its ugly head again. For many, engaging in smoking cannabis can clearly enhance their standing within a social group. There is a tendency for boys to exaggerate their use of cannabis and their expertise in the range of ways they take it. What is more, as in many other activities, they make fun of other boys who cannot handle it. But it goes deeper than that. A drug education team working in Lancashire conducted a huge survey into boys' use of cannabis and discovered what is a rather sad indictment, and also the main reason that boys were saying they smoked cannabis – that it enabled them to relax, be themselves and talk to their friends. What they would miss most of all, should they stop smoking cannabis, was their ability to relax with their friends.

> In 2002, a New Zealand study showed that those who started using cannabis by the time they were 18 had a four-fold increase in the risk of developing schizophrenia-like illness by the age of 26. The areas of the adolescent brain associated with motivation, impulsivity and addiction are still rapidly developing, which may mean that teenagers are more vulnerable to the addictive and psychotic actions of drugs they take at what is a crucial stage in neural development.
>
> *Dr Raj Persaud (2005)*

Barrier 23

Low self-esteem and limiting self-beliefs

People outside education, particularly those who do not have sons of their own, often fail to recognize that, for many boys, low self-esteem is an issue. They are often thrown by boys' ebullience or the 'front' that they project. Likewise, the complexity of self-esteem is often misunderstood. It is not something like a broken finger that will mend itself, or that can be quickly fixed. The following represents a useful breakdown of the various elements of self-esteem.

> Self-esteem is a composite of six vital ingredients that can empower or detract from the vitality of our lives:
>
> **PHYSICAL SAFETY**
> Freedom from physical harm.
>
> **EMOTIONAL SECURITY**
> The absence of intimidations and fears.
>
> **IDENTITY**
> The 'Who am I?' question.
>
> **AFFILIATION**
> A sense of belonging.
>
> **COMPETENCE**
> A sense of feeling capable.
>
> **MISSION**
> The feeling that one's life has meaning and direction.
>
> *(B.B. Youngs in Dryden and Vos 2001)*

Take the example of a dual heritage boy in an insensitive environment who might be suffering racist slurs from two communities. It is clear that his sense of physical safety, emotional security and identity will feature significantly in his developing self-esteem. Schools have to ask themselves how they are going to address these issues and raise the self-esteem of such young people. One in 25 pupils in Key Stage 1 is now of dual or shared heritage, and the numbers are steadily growing each year. Dual and shared heritage pupils are the fastest growing section of the school population. How quickly is the realization of this fact growing? How rapidly are schools growing in their awareness of the factors involved? How quickly are schools developing an understanding of what they can do to make a difference to the developing self-esteem of pupils who may be in the situation as described? Schools have to represent the cultures that are presented in their school in their very fabric, in the curriculum, in staffing at all levels and in terms of parental involvement. It can no longer be purely in a decorative sense through occasional assemblies and exotic displays. There has to be, to begin with, a greater understanding of and engagement with the issues by adults involved with the life of the school.

So what of the self-esteem of the Year 8 boy who is in bottom set humanities on a Friday afternoon and, subsequently, in the bottom set for at least half the week because that is how the timetable works? What are his issues around affiliation with the rest of school? Or his mission? Or perhaps above all – his competence? It would appear on the surface that the answer to this particular problem is quite straightforward, isn't it? Surely we need to face up to the big question of how much disaffection we might get rid of were we to group all pupils positively rather than just a chosen few. How much would, for example, going mixed ability or even parallel grouping increase levels of self-esteem?

 box

> I came across a school recently where a small group of Year 9 borderline level 5 boys had been summoned together for a programme of intensive mentoring. Upon arriving at the room where the first meeting was taking place one boy noticed that written on the board in large capitals was the legend 'THE HIDDEN TALENT GROUP'. With a smile on his face the boy asked, 'Does that mean I'm not thick then miss?'

So many of our underachieving boys are recognizable simply from the way they walk, stand or hold their head. Their underachievement, you might say, is written all over them! The self-fulfilling prophecy is not only the domain of teachers or parents who might say 'Well what do you expect from a group of lads like that!' or 'Well what do you expect, he's a boy.' A boy, indeed! Anyone, in fact, is quite capable of talking himself into no end of underachievement. Because they feel the way they do about their chances, they are more likely to just go along with anything that will confirm themselves to be right in their beliefs. Ultimately, they just bring about what they always expected to happen. It might not always be clear where these self-limiting beliefs come from, but we do know why we should get rid of them.

 box

Negative self-talk even changes your physiology

- Ask pupils to choose a partner and stand side by side.
- Ask 'A' to raise their arm straight out in front of them, parallel with their shoulders and with their palm flat.
- Ask them to repeat their name out loud in a clear strong voice, over and over again.
- After a few minutes ask 'B' to use both hands to apply pressure to A's arm to push it down by their side and notice how much pressure it takes (usually quite a lot!).
- Repeat the exercise, this time with 'A' repeating, in a rather glum fashion, 'I can't play the saxophone.'
- Again, after a few minutes B needs to apply the pressure, noticing the difference (invariably quite significant).

Help pupils to identify and eliminate their negative self-talk as a way of engendering positive self-belief. Give them a challenging mental task that on the surface looks quite simple, such as the one below.

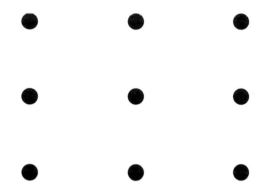

Without taking your pen off the paper, draw four straight lines that pass through all nine dots.

Ask the children to do it quietly on their own and, as they struggle with the task, ask them to listen to the voice in their head. What is it saying to them? What is its tone? How is it making them feel? You might even ask them to write the words down to see how ridiculous they look on paper. Then ask the children to ceremoniously tear them up! If you feel they can handle it, ask them to all say the words out loud over and over again in the most ridiculous voices they can manage, to hear for themselves how ludicrous they sound. You might even ask them to keep a diary for homework of all the negative things they tell themselves over the course of a week! Now ask them to make a selection of the statements that they have used against themselves and then think of the precise opposites. 'I'm useless at...' will become 'I'm really very good at ... and improving all the time.' These are well known as positive affirmations, the generally accepted rules for which are that such affirmations must be wholly positive, in the present tense, written down and repeated frequently. Positive affirmations can be a real beginning, but the most powerful process is developing a whole new internal voice. The process requires locating precisely where the voice comes from, focusing hard on changing its tone to a confident and positive one and changing what it is saying from negative criticism to positive encouragement. This is a well-understood process in the field of self-improvement that so many adults are exploring. Is there any reason why we should not share these ideas with those in our care whose limiting self-beliefs are seriously threatening their life chances?

Info **box**

Pioneering work in schools devised and led by International Leadership Consultant Sandra Smethurst (www.sandrasmethurst.com) and supported by holistic practitioners Vital Connections and myself has included a day's workshop for large groups of pupils, planned out as follows:

- developing a sense of emotional well-being through a wide range of breathing and simple yoga exercises
- the visualization of goals
- empowerment exercises
- the identification of self-limiting beliefs
- breaking through the barriers – in a range of ways – sometimes including breaking through pine boards.

What we focus on expands in our lives. We are literally creating our own reality. If at the beginning of the day we are expecting to have a tough day, then there is every chance that is exactly what we will have, as we will focus on those elements that are likely to make our day 'tough' and more will manifest themselves. A good example of this would be if we were considering buying ourselves a new blue mini, almost everywhere we looked we would suddenly see blue minis. With many underachieving boys, wherever they look they see ways that prove their lack of worth, their lack of ability and a range of manifestations of their underachievement. If we were to clear the filters that restrict what is flowing in, then the haze would clear and they would gain a wider perception of life, a broader vision of what is possible. To do this we desperately need to replace their self-limiting beliefs with a sense of real belief.

 box

Self-belief exercise

Ask everyone to stand, feet together and arms by their sides.

Tell them to raise one arm parallel to their shoulder, and point straight ahead. They now need to keep their feet still but move their pointed arm to the right, as far as they can go, then note where they pointed to on the wall behind them. Ask them to return to their original position but this time close their eyes and just IMAGINE that they are repeating the exercise. 'Imagine that you are moving your arm round to the right, a bit further, a little bit further, and then instead of stopping, you carry on. In fact ... you end up round the front. Unbelievable!' Ask them to IMAGINE the process once more.

Ask them to open their eyes and then repeat the actual process, noting where they reach the second time. Everyone will get further. Now ask them what it means.

One seven-year-old boy's hand shot straight up in the air when we had all done the exercise in assembly. 'It means that if you think you can do something then you can!' 'Well done young Henry Ford,' was my response. For it was, indeed, he that originated the thought.

The front of a postcard that was sent in May 2005 to all Year 11 students about to sit their GCSEs in Kirklees Local Authority contained not a hard-working, 'biddable' girl, but a fairly uncompromising picture of a young man, complete with the 'Believe' campaign wristband. On the reverse I wrote a list of tips which did not just encompass the practical, making reference to the basics, including the importance of reading questions carefully, but also included reminders about the importance of feeling good in order to do well. In this sense, the reminders were about not only eating healthily and keeping hydrated but also about emotional health and well-being. The card reinforced other elements of the campaign, which included staff training in relaxation techniques, breathing exercises, visualization and positive affirmations. It stressed, in particular, the importance of self-belief and the need to avoid those who might exert a negative influence. It was awarded a Plain English Campaign award for its direct and clear approach.

**Good luck in the coming days
Here are some last minute expert tips!**

- The night before picture yourself in the exam, doing really well and smiling!
- Have an early night
- Have a high-energy breakfast
- Pick up your free snack and bottle of water
- Avoid people who moan and complain!
- Believe in yourself!
- Relax and breathe deeply to the count of three, three times
- 66% of poor marks are because of careless reading so read questions carefully
- Highlight keywords in questions
- Stretch and breathe deeply between answers
- Show them what you know ... really go for it
- Check it through carefully to pick up extra marks
- Congratulate yourself on a job well done!

With our very best wishes
Gavin Tonkin, Director of Lifelong Learning and Cllr Kath Pinnock, Leader of Kirklees Council

Barrier 24

Lack of engagement with the life of the school

In primary schools, it is extremely common to see boys in charge of the library, the ICT suite, the office at lunchtime or even in charge of the headteacher! In many schools, they may be the head's PA or young executives or whatever, with fancy badges, their photographs up in the entrance hall and training for their roles and responsibilities delivered by the head or a senior member of staff. Upon arrival at the high school it has been known, in the dim and distant past, for the young executive to turn up and ask 'What do you want me to do sir?', only to be told 'I want you to sit down, shut up and get on with it! That's what I want you to do' (the three-part lesson). But not any more, we hope. It virtually goes without saying that pupil engagement with the life of the school can enhance their success as a learner, not least as it enhances the development of self-esteem and, potentially, their motivation.

In the high school, it is fairly well understood that boys who have achieved a high status in school sport, can, if they so wish, also get away with working hard. The fact that they are 'one of the lads' on the sports field means that they have been granted a licence to achieve elsewhere. For many of these, it can be argued, they are actively engaged in the life of the school. There are, however, many more who are not. There are many who are there out of sufferance and when asked what they like about school reply 'break time', 'the tennis courts' or 'seeing my mates'.

How can we actively engage boys in the life of the school in ways other than sport? We could start by listening to them far more – that could really help! We do not possess a culture in this country of adults listening to children. It has to change. School councils can provide the opportunity for that engagement, particularly when handed a reasonable budget and given the opportunity to deal with a meaty agenda, such as discipline, uniform, school meals, reward systems, bullying and so on. 'Friday parliament', in one school that I am aware of, engaged many youngsters actively, not only in the life of the school but also in current affairs and life in the local community. 'Investors in Pupils' is a recent innovation whereby schools can receive recognition for the extent to which they actively give pupils a voice in their own learning. As a visitor to many schools, I invariably choose to listen to lots of boys to see exactly what their perceptions are of the place where they spend so much of their formative years.

box

The school tour: where would your visitors be led?

Being taken around a school by a couple of Year 11 boys is invariably an education! On one such visit I asked them to take me to points of interest, telling them I had limited time available. First port of call was the dining room. Idly remarking that it resembled a fast-food outlet, replete with photographs of the kind of food you would like to think you were getting, I was quickly put to rights: 'It's not like that at all sir, in fact the school council regularly discusses the food that is served and how we can provide a healthy diet.' The second port of call was the CDT area. The display was staggering. Every square inch of wall on the corridor was filled with coursework. A whole wall was given over to an A* folder of work, and next to it a giant 'A*'. Similarly, another wall featured a C folder, with a giant 'C' emblazoned next to it. The boys stood there, eyeing the work, waiting for my next blundering comment.

'So you like this then?' I asked, cagily, 'Why?'
'Well without it we wouldn't know what an A* really looks like, would we?'

Third stop was the corridor outside the RE department, where happy, smiling pictures of pupils adorned a huge display. Unlike any other pictures of pupils in the building, these were on a meaningful, eye-catching scale. Seeing their two grinning faces appearing from the midst of the display, I did not need to ask any more dumb questions. It was obvious that here were two boys who were proud to be part of their school, have their voices heard, their needs met and their successes celebrated.

Engaging pupils at any age in research in schools can have huge benefits. On several occasions I have organized groups of primary-aged boys to conduct research across the whole school on the differences between boys' and girls' reading habits. They formulated the questions, interviewed all the pupils in school then collated the findings. They presented these in graph form, with accompanying commentary in assembly.

box

What we found out

- Twice as many girls as boys get books for presents.
- Nearly everyone we asked said they always read the book from the library.
- About half the school, particularly the girls, felt they weren't allowed to use the library enough.
- Twice as many girls as boys used the mobile library.
- Nearly everyone said they enjoyed reading.
- But a lot more girls said they read for at least half an hour a day.
- Nearly everyone said they read at least one book a week.
- Nearly every girl said they prefer stories to non-fiction.
- A third of the boys prefer non-fiction.

What I tend to find is fairly common is that when pupils do the research, unlike many adults, they tend to like to see something happen as a result of their endeavours. In the same school, the following were the outcomes.

 box

The ideas the group came up with after the research

- Full school reading weeks.
- Tell parents that books for presents is a good idea.
- Have competitions with books as prizes.
- Give books as rewards for good work.
- Ask the head if we can use the school library more.
- Ask the mobile library librarian to talk to school.
- Have reading challenges.
- Have internet in library.
- Buy parents books for presents.
- Let parents borrow books from the library or have their own book swap shelves in entrance.

Chickenly J, I and N

As suggested previously there are many key areas of school activity where it is vital to engage boys if we wish to raise their levels of achievement. Reading is just one of them. The research suggested earlier into how significant a currency your reward system represents for boys in your school can also be a critical use of the pupil voice to enhance boys' engagement with the life of the school. Involvement in the development of school policies around issues such as bullying, sexual harassment, racism and homophobia occurs more and more in schools, to the benefit not only of the boys but also of the school community. Where boys are asked to engage with looking at the nature of breaks and lunchtimes, the potential for ensuring the provision of boy-friendly activities beyond sport is clearly increased. Where boys are engaged in selecting new fiction for the library, male readers may increase in numbers. Not exactly rocket science, but it is fair to say that taking pupils' voices into account is not something that comes to us readily.

 box

Asked to take photographs of areas around the school that particularly inspired or interested them, a small group of infant children dutifully tottered off to do as they were bid. One small boy returned with his digital photograph. Delighted that the boy had so obviously been inspired by the sensory garden that was the teacher's pride and joy, adorned with all manner of wind chimes and hangings, and a range of textured surfaces, she waxed lyrical for some time about the boy's wonderful choice. When asked for his comments, the boy pointed to the, as yet, rather underdeveloped area next to it, an expanse of nothingness, 'No, miss, it's the mud, I love the mud.'

Barrier 25

Homophobic bullying

Homophobia is widely used by boys in particular as a way of policing what is acceptable and what is unacceptable male behaviour and, as such, can affect more than non-heterosexual boys. Whenever or wherever it is felt to be fashionable to use the term 'gay', it is often used to describe the kind of things that REAL boys do not do, such as work hard or care about things or have feelings. In this context alone, it is hugely unhelpful as it represents another very powerful weapon in the peer police's armoury. In terms of its impact on lesbian, gay and bisexual (LGB) young people, the problem is considerably more significant. The *Stand Up For Us* report (HDA nd) is full of testimonies of young people. The author shared with me his experience of a discussion with a group of extremely intelligent and articulate 16-year-old boys and his dismay upon discovering that not a single one of them was going on to further or higher education. All of them cited their experiences at school as the reason. It was not just the experience of name calling and bullying by other students that had resulted in this decision either.

The worst thing about homophobia in my school is knowing that the teachers won't stop it. They pretend it isn't happening, some even join in. It's bad enough without teachers patronizing you by saying things like "it'll go away" or "we don't hear anyone saying anything".

Boy, Year 9

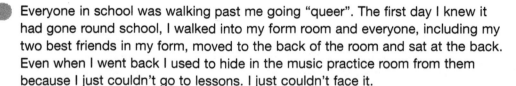

Everyone in school was walking past me going "queer". The first day I knew it had gone round school, I walked into my form room and everyone, including my two best friends in my form, moved to the back of the room and sat at the back. Even when I went back I used to hide in the music practice room from them because I just couldn't go to lessons. I just couldn't face it.

Young man, aged 18

Pupils who are victims of homophobic bullying:

- have higher levels of absenteeism and truancy
- are less likely to enter higher or further education
- are more likely to contemplate self-harm and suicide.

More than 40 per cent of LGB men and women who had been bullied at school made at least one attempt to self-harm, while more than 20 per cent had attempted suicide (Rivers 2001; Mullen 1999).

Another disturbing statistic and, in the light of the above, perhaps the most disturbing statistic of all, are the findings of the DfES in 2002. Investigating bullying policies, they identified the fact that while almost all schools had anti-bullying policies, only six per cent referred specifically to homophobic bullying. Stonewall is an organization dedicated to, among other things, eradicating homophobic bullying in schools. They report that four in five high school teachers are aware of verbal bullying and one in four is aware of physical homophobic bullying. Postcards produced by Stonewall (available from www.stonewall.org.uk) are a useful way of collating pupil and adult feedback on the current level of incidence of homophobic bullying.

Stand Up For Us provides guidelines as to how to engage governors, involve children and young people in an audit and begin to challenge stereotypes. The report fulfils all staff training needs in the preparation of rewriting and effectively operating school bullying policies incorporating homophobia. This clearly needs to be a priority in schools where no such policy exists.

 Teachers with street cred need to stand up for us; if you have respect for your teacher what they say is OK.

Young man, aged 16

Parents' lack of understanding of the role that they can play

Parents should be saying to their children that school is where you go to learn to become a giant.

Dr Richard Majors

There is nothing wrong with having an ideal such as the above, although it is clear that many parents' own experiences of school often jaundice the ways in which they show their support for their own children's school. When a parent is saying, 'Yeah I know school's rubbish, I hated it when I was your age, but you've got to go otherwise I'll be in trouble with the law!' it hardly bodes well for a fruitful home–school partnership. It is also the case that some schools are themselves less than welcoming:

Hotels in the 1930s and 1940s were once described as theatres of humiliation for some guests. For some parents today, some schools are precisely that.

Phil Street OBE, ContinYou

Sometimes, and this is certainly the case within the context of raising boys' achievement, I believe that we quite simply have to bridge those gaps. In the mid-1990s at the school where I was working, I felt that despite all our best efforts to have an impact on boys' attitude, behaviour and subsequently their performance, there were many things beyond our control. I decided we had to talk to parents about our concerns and we should do this by holding a parents' conference. A letter was carefully worded, to engage and motivate! And, most importantly, it was sent to all parents in all our feeder primary schools

Let's make the boys shine

A lot of boys don't...

✓ do as well in tests as girls do
✓ read as much as girls do
✓ work as neatly as girls do
✓ like doing homework
✓ organize themselves very well
✓ come prepared to lessons
✓ work hard in case they're made fun of
✓ work too hard when they're young but expect to do well at sixteen

The truth is it shows...

✓ boys are doing less well than girls in almost every exam

What are we going to do about it?

Parents' conference
23 March 7.30pm at the High School

It did the trick. Seventy-five parents attended, mostly mums (more on this later!). A local drama group were invited to produce a short drama piece to help break the ice. The depiction of stereotypical boy behaviour from a 'Kevin' (an indolent adolescent from the then popular *Harry Enfield Show*), coupled with hapless and despairing parents certainly achieved that! The ensuing discussion brought the focus squarely on what the serious implications were for boys. Selecting a group to work with, with people they knew and a friendly teacher, the 75 parents directed their attention towards what parents might do. Each group was charged with the responsibility of coming up with a number of tips for other parents.

WHAT CAN PARENTS DO?

Five helpful hints

Some of the ideas they came up with included:

1 *Give lots of encouragement to boost confidence. Having your own system of rewards at home can also help.*

   The discussion highlighted what most parents felt – that while all children needed encouragement and praise, boys particularly needed it since they appeared to be getting more than their fair share of negative attention! As far as the rewards are concerned, short term is best.

2 *Guide him towards out-of-school activities that he will not only enjoy, but at which he can also succeed.*

   This came from a heartfelt plea from one mum who described a not uncommon occurrence. Dad would be taking his eight-year-old son to the local under 9s football team, reliving his own footballing glory days vicariously, and the boy would be one of the permanent reserves, on the touchline in the hail and snow, his confidence and self-esteem sapping away on a weekly basis.

3 *Give him more responsibilities around the house and do not do everything for him!*

   The big one, and the one that all the parents insisted ought to be printed in bold letters. Shocking as it may seem, some mums were saying they were still packing their sons' bags at the age of 15 and 16!

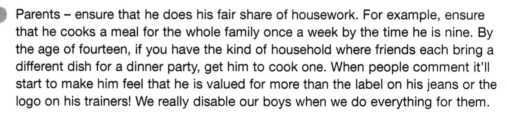

Parents – ensure that he does his fair share of housework. For example, ensure that he cooks a meal for the whole family once a week by the time he is nine. By the age of fourteen, if you have the kind of household where friends each bring a different dish for a dinner party, get him to cook one. When people comment it'll start to make him feel that he is valued for more than the label on his jeans or the logo on his trainers! We really disable our boys when we do everything for them.

Steven Biddulph on his 'Talking tour' 2005

4 *Try to create some learning opportunities for learning at home by discussing the news or television programmes.*

   The point was well made at the meeting that children were at school for only about 15 per cent of their week and that there were clearly hundreds of learning opportunities that were being missed.

5 *Persuade him that talking over problems is best, as it can help release tension and anger.*

   Parents were very clear on the difficulties in getting lots of boys to do this and are keen to get help and advice.

6 *Check his student planner regularly (if he has one) and also ...*

7 *Make sure he has a list of things he needs for school each day and make sure he gets himself properly organized in time. 'Planning and preparation prevent poor performance!'*

   Continuing the big message to parents about avoiding the creation of 'learned helplessness' and ensuring that he is getting himself organized.

8 *Contact school immediately if you feel that your son might be under pressure not to work.*

The often devastating impact of the anti-swot or anti-boff culture on boys' achievement is not as clearly understood by parents as it is by teachers. It needs explaining and it requires vigilance on their part.

9 *If your son has a reading habit, encourage it. If not, do your best to help him develop one. You could ask his teacher's advice. Seeing other males in the house reading can also help.*

The mums present clearly stated that most of their partners read little, except perhaps newspapers or instruction manuals. They also admitted that they had been the ones who had done all the bedtime reading. It was also an issue that in order to get their boys reading, they did not have a clue what to buy – hence the reference to guidance from their teachers.

10 *Good male role models in the family can play a hugely significant part in boys' education; for example, by reading to them, giving help and advice with work at home or even by helping out at school.*

Helping at home, given the motivation and the right guidance, might be a possibility, helping at school can be more complex, but successful projects and partnerships do exist all over the country (see below).

These tips and many more became a leaflet (see opposite) that has been successfully used at new intake evenings at both high schools and primary schools. Most effective, I believe, because the tips did not come from the government, or the local authority, or even from teachers, but from parents themselves.

 box

Projects and partnerships

'It's a Man Thing' project, focusing on reading, writing and helping encourage fathers to become more active in their children's learning, has been run in Derbyshire, Dudley, Hereford, Bradford, Coventry, Newham and Portsmouth.

The Youth Sports Trust with community learning charity ContinYou runs a 'Top Dads' project in schools across the country to introduce young fathers to sport-related play, while offering one-to-one and small group mentoring guidance on positive parenting.

ContinYou's 'Active Dads' project runs in schools across Britain to help fathers and other male carers engage with their children through a variety of activities including reading, walking and going on trips to leisure centres or places of local interest. In Lancashire, cricket-loving boys and their fathers are loaned cricket kit, books and activity cards, and encouraged to read together as well as play sport.

Cookery clubs designed to improve communications skills between dads and their children operate in various parts of the country.

All over the country there are:

- Lads and Dads Book Clubs
- Fathers and sons conferences
- Schools 'Adopting a granddad'
- Bring Dad to School Days
- Dads groups that meet to discuss parenting issues
- Saturday morning computer clubs for fathers and sons

Any of these sound familiar?

- The papers are full of stories about how boys don't do as well in tests as girls do.
- Teachers say boys aren't as interested in reading as girls.
- Teachers often say boys aren't as organised as girls.
- Teachers say that boys are often let down by their writing skills.
- Boys sometimes say "I don't need to work hard - I know it all anyway" or "I'll catch up later."
- Boys sometimes get bullied by other boys simply because they work hard.
- Boys sometimes treat girls badly just to make themselves feel better.

Yes? So what can we do about it?

Parents working hand in hand with schools can really help...

What about the girls?

Experience shows that girls benefit from any work that is done to improve the way boys work and behave.

Kirklees
EDUCATION SERVICE

Parents from local schools gathered together to listen to the facts about boys' underachievement and then discussed ways that they felt parents might make a difference.

This leaflet is based on original ideas from parents from the Newsome Pyramid of schools in Kirklees. If you have any comments or helpful hints to add, contact: Gary Wilson, The Raising Boys' Achievement Co-ordinator, School Effectiveness Service, The Deighton Centre, Deighton Road, Huddersfield HD2 1HG

Let's Hear it for the Boys

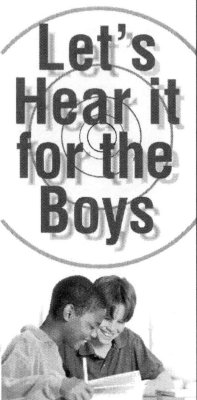

How to help...

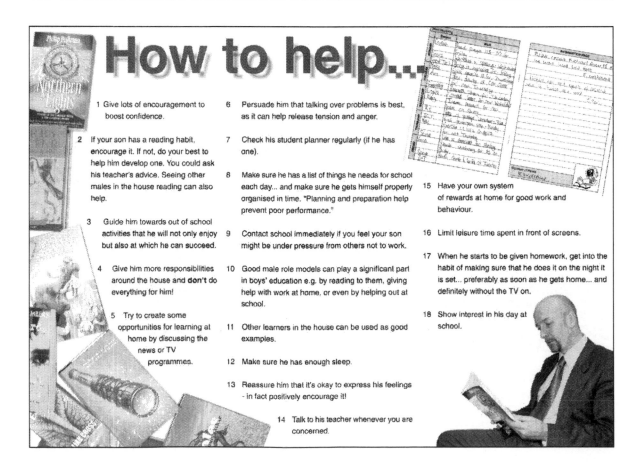

1 Give lots of encouragement to boost confidence.

2 If your son has a reading habit, encourage it. If not, do your best to help him develop one. You could ask his teacher's advice. Seeing other males in the house reading can also help.

3 Guide him towards out of school activities that he will not only enjoy but also at which he can succeed.

4 Give him more responsibilities around the house and **don't** do everything for him!

5 Try to create some opportunities for learning at home by discussing the news or TV programmes.

6 Persuade him that talking over problems is best, as it can help release tension and anger.

7 Check his student planner regularly (if he has one).

8 Make sure he has a list of things he needs for school each day... and make sure he gets himself properly organised in time. "Planning and preparation help prevent poor performance."

9 Contact school immediately if you feel your son might be under pressure from others not to work.

10 Good male role models can play a significant part in boys' education e.g. by reading to them, giving help with work at home, or even by helping out at school.

11 Other learners in the house can be used as good examples.

12 Make sure he has enough sleep.

13 Reassure him that it's okay to express his feelings - in fact positively encourage it!

14 Talk to his teacher whenever you are concerned.

15 Have your own system of rewards at home for good work and behaviour.

16 Limit leisure time spent in front of screens.

17 When he starts to be given homework, get into the habit of making sure that he does it on the night it is set... preferably as soon as he gets home... and definitely without the TV on.

18 Show interest in his day at school.

Subsequently, many schools I have worked with have developed their own leaflets for parents, often with information from key departments as to how they can best support the completion of coursework for example, encourage the use of appropriate online or other revision support materials, or how they might best understand their son's preferred learning style and therefore be able to support their studying more effectively.

At one of the boys' conferences that I organized, one workshop consisted of a group of Year 6 boys producing an article for the council's parent magazine; below is an extract:

> We are a group of boys who would just like to say that we are nothing like the bad picture painted. On the whole we are motivated and want to achieve and we have some advice for parents who want to help their boys have the same attitude to school as we do. Boys are not different to girls, because we are all humans. Consider how you treat your son and how you treat your daughter. Do you give your son as much responsibility as your daughter? If you don't isn't it time that you did? In order to get more from boys, parents must talk about our school day, check homework and sign homework diaries. We also think it is important for parents to provide us with a quiet place to do our homework. Also, make sure we have limited time watching the television or playing computer games, so we don't become couch potatoes! Help us to organize ourselves by making us sort out our own bags. If we forget, it's our own fault. In future life who is going to help us?
>
> To conclude, we feel parents should give us boys responsibilities. Talk to us and generally be a support in this really important area of our lives. If this happens, then perhaps the newspapers and teachers would start to see boys in a good light. We can achieve, we can do well, if our parents are behind us.

Worth a try?

The importance of allowing boys to develop independence from an early age is one of the most significant points that is necessary to stress to parents. However, within some cultures it is anathema to give young boys responsibilities of any kind. They are regarded as young princes. As part of an ancient cultural and religious tradition, it is not appropriate to criticize and condemn. It is, however, I believe still necessary to draw the parallels between becoming independent and becoming an independent and effective learner. A few years ago, I asked someone who had worked for 25 years within precisely those communities, what advice he would give to parents of boys, he said to me:

> Tell them...
>
> "Mums, say no and make sure you mean it. Eighty per cent of your son's teachers will be female, and if he won't listen to you, he won't listen to them."
>
> And tell them....
>
> "We'll not get racism out of this country until your sons and daughters become lawyers."
>
> And wherever you go, you must say...
>
> "...and get them to bed at night."

And so I do.

The need for adult males in the home to spend time with boys is an issue within all communities. The latest groups in need of this message are those parents who may be money rich but often time poor. So much time is spent by parents of boys pushing and pulling them in the direction of the door first thing in the morning and the direction of their homework first thing in the evening. I suggest for the parents of boys that 'less tugging and more hugging' would probably be far better, combined with a commitment to searching for opportunities to praise not just academic achievements but all achievements. Comparing the number of times parents tell off their sons with the number of times they praise them is a useful exercise to pass on to parents. If teachers have an understanding of the power of the three (positive) to one (negative) rule, then why not share this with parents? Parents need to understand, too, that they need to always respond to their son's questioning otherwise he will stop asking questions. Conversely, we often need to teach parents exactly how they might approach questioning their sons if they wish to avoid a cursory grunt. Open questioning is a skill that, as teachers, we can pass on. In Alistair Smith and Bill Lucas' *How to Help Your Child Succeed* (2002), they even offer the 'script' that parents might use in order to help their child. The fact that some phrases might be the kind parents may use through gritted teeth is irrelevant! They represent real practical guidance. Where else might it come from?

Coaching your child with R..E..S..P..E..C..T..
- Reassuring: 'I know you thought this would be a good way of doing this and...'
- Enthusiastic: 'I really like the way you...'
- Steady: 'That's okay. I'll wait while you pick them all up again.'
- Practical: 'Let's see what happens when we try this again...'
- Engaging: 'I'll do it first, then you try.'
- Clear: 'When you move your hand more slowly, you will stop smudging your writing.'
- Truthful: 'You're not as good at kicking with your left foot as your right, so we should practise.'

(Smith and Lucas 2002)

I have previously mentioned the fact that we have very young children in our care who know far more about what is good for them than their parents do. The only way that we can ensure that our messages are consolidated and not constantly undermined is to develop a dialogue. All communities are different of course. While some might need a meeting or two, some gentle reminders and tips, others may demand significantly more.

The newly appointed head of Mitchell High School in Stoke, for example, decided in 2002 that the only way she was going to raise the self-esteem of the young people in her charge was by raising the self-esteem of their parents. At the time the school was achieving less than 10 per cent 5A*–Cs. First of all, she and other staff spent lots of time talking to parents, engaging them, in small ways at first, in the life of the school. Subsequently, through the Pacific Institute's 'Steps' courses for parents and young people, they became fixtures in the school. The development of a Community Learning Centre meant that currently about 700 parents have some kind of active involvement with the school, and the school's 5A*–Cs in 2005 were almost 50 per cent. One parent, Donna, describes her experience:

> The Donna that I used to be was nasty, aggressive, wouldn't take no for an answer, always wanted to see the head. If I felt anyone had had a go at my boys, I wanted to come straight in. I would believe anything they would say ... I'd had a nervous breakdown and I had an aggressive partner into drugs ... he'd been to prison ... Then I kept having phone calls from the school to come in and do a social care course. Then later I did a Steps course and realized there was a me. My self-talk is "I can do it".
>
> My boys were pains – they were the problem, not the teachers. I wouldn't have ever known if I hadn't come in. They went on a 'Go For It' residential course and they came back completely different. The school has turned our whole lives around – the boys would not be where they are today if it hadn't been for Mitchell.

Donna later became a dinner lady, worked in the in-school exclusion unit and ultimately became a learning mentor. In 2005, she was presented with the Adult Learner of the Year Award at the Albert Hall.

Barrier 27

Intervention occurring too late

It is still not uncommon for intervention to occur as late as Year 10 or even Year 11, and often just with the boys who are borderline C/Ds. The truth is the boys on the borderline are exhibiting signs far earlier than that and we must begin, as they say, at the beginning.

Prior to starting school it is important to help develop an understanding in parents as to how significant the role of older males in the family can be, not least in reading, questioning and talking but also in terms of presenting a positive role model to boys.

At the outset of schooling, parents need reminding of the importance of encouraging the development of independence in order that their boy becomes an independent and effective learner.

In the early years, teachers need to ensure that the peer police cadets do not begin to exert a stranglehold on the development of caring, creative and engaged young boys.

At the same time we need to be applying far more sensitivity during the early stages of developing boys' reading and writing, and giving more time for learning through structured play.

As they pass through primary school, immediate attention has to be given and appropriate strategies applied as and when required to those whose literary skills are identified as lacking.

Shortly after transition to the high school, signs of underachievement arising from peer pressure, disaffection or low self-esteem need to be recognized and acted upon.

If mentoring is to be used, Year 8 is a good time to begin, not Year 11. Pupil tracking systems allow for far earlier recognition of academic underperformance than they have ever done before. We need to act upon the information they provide us.

Teachers' lack of awareness of the barriers to boys' learning

But not you any more! Now that you have hopefully achieved a clearer picture of the complexity of the issue, you are now officially a national expert!

The question that remains is not 'Why do boys underachieve?' or 'What can we do about it?' but 'Where do you start?'. The quick answer is with the grid that can be found in Appendix 1 (see pages 137–140). The 28 barriers to boys' achievement are presented there in chart form to be utilized by schools in whatever groupings seem appropriate. In primary contexts, this might be whole school, senior management team or by Key Stage. In high schools, it might be senior management, subject leaders, pastoral teams or subject departments.

Whatever groups are considered to be most appropriate, the activity that I recommend is the same. Taking the chart as a tool, identify in groups which barriers specifically impact on boys in your area of work. The barriers that you identify as having the greatest impact should be given the highest priority for action. The chart allows you to select between 1 (top priority) and 5 (low priority). The recommendation would then be to select no more than five high priority areas for action for your Key Stage, subject area, pastoral team or whole-school action plan. The chart may also be a useful place to begin to note down those strategies, some of which you have found here, that do match the particular barriers that require your attention. Noting who might be responsible would be a further useful step to take at this point.

The whole-school model

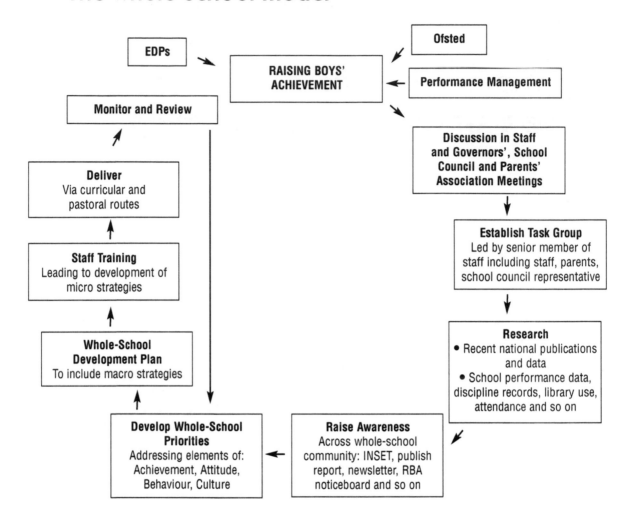

Adopting the whole-school development model, one school that I worked with as part of a LPSA (Local Public Service Agreement) project addressed the issue in their school over a period of three years. Beginning with a range of discussions in a range of groups, senior management, student groups, governors and so on, it was determined that the school set up a project group. The group consisted of eight staff, broadly representing all major subject areas within the school. The first step they chose to take was to plan a whole-school INSET on the issue. I presented the INSET day and the project teams chose to run a series of workshops on what were considered to be priorities for the school. These included teaching and learning, coursework and so on. The follow-up to the day involved the whole staff in the 'Barriers to Boys' Learning' exercise, which subsequently enabled them to highlight their priority areas and hand them to the project team for research and development over the following three years.

Classroom strategies adopted included:

● A strong focus on teaching and learning/and the development of the Gold Standard Lesson which included:
  ● a strong emphasis on the presentation of clear outcomes
  ● a variety of tasks (VAK)
  ● lots of opportunities for reflection.

- A focus on coursework, including the introduction of 'chunking down' and letters to parents showing them how they could support their boys. After-school revision sessions were also established.

- The use of Year 7 and Year 10 calendared tutorial time to explore preferred learning styles and matching strategies to improve their own learning.

- A focus on interactions with boys and girls in lesson observations – both management and peer.

- The introduction of shared reading, using older, less confident boys teaching younger boys to read.

- The effective display of exemplar work.

- Learning to Learn course for Year 8.

- Introduction of Philosophy for Children.

- Reading weeks – five lessons per half term (first lesson in the day for five days every half term).

Whole-school strategies adopted included:

- The introduction of mentoring Year 8 and Year 10 (including group mentoring and in addition to existing Year 11 mentoring).

- The development of a Year 6 newsletter, sharing achievements, giving helpful settling-in advice and so on.

- Achievement displays/photos that took on a new scale, standard of professionalism and emphasis.

- Target setting/monitoring made more rigorous via in-school training on assessment – formative assessment, databases and use of data to enhance attainment.

- The purchase of Trackmaster software to facilitate student monitoring.

- The introduction of interim levels to assist target setting in Year 7 and Year 8.

- The librarian's attendance at an LEA course – 'Developing a boy-friendly library'.

- Increased staff supervision at lunchtime to improve atmosphere during/after lunch – free lunch for staff.

- Visits made to other schools' training days on Thinking Skills, Boys' literacy, Boys' self-esteem.

- Online questionnaires to Year 8 and Year 10 re boys' perceptions of school.

- Re-addressing the school's cross-curricular literacy policy to promote more speaking/listening activities.

- The introduction of praise postcards/phone calls home.

Cross-phase strategies developed included:

- Improving links with Key Stage 2 PSHCE, which in turn led to better induction.

- Whole cluster parents' evening focusing on how to support boys in their learning.

- Whole cluster Big Arts Day to actively promote to boys about to enter the high school for the first time, how much the high school valued boys who were predisposed to expressive, creative and performing arts.

- Development of a range of cross-phase activities.

- Development of a Primary Learning Network to raise boys' achievements in writing.

As one of a group of five schools, later expanding to ten, the school also had the benefit of:

- half-termly project leaders' meetings
- sharing action plans and strategies
- sharing residuals across schools to identify boy-friendly practice
- termly heads' meetings
- visits to other schools
- contributing to and sharing a newsletter for the whole LEA
- raising boys' achievement website.

It is important to note that this is by no means an exhaustive list of the work the school carried out. Neither does this in any way represent a recipe for success for any other school. Every school, indeed every cohort of boys, is entirely unique and demands careful analysis prior to action. The school described above, however, did significantly reduce its gender gap and remains the only school in the authority where examination results have improved year on year for the last seven years.

Key features of the LPSA project in the ten schools that were universally valued were the numerous opportunities to share good practice over almost half of the LEA's high schools. Not least among these were the successes many of the schools were having with:

- The development of whole-school literacy initiatives related to structuring boys' writing, increasing speaking and listening opportunities and so on.
- Whole-school reading weeks, designed primarily to give boys a 'licence to read' and help develop their skills of reflection.
- 'Chunking' coursework, in order to approach it in a 'boy-friendly way' that is, in short chunks, with short-term goals and short-term rewards.
- The growth in understanding of the importance of appropriate teaching and learning styles.
- Closer attention given to the clear indication of learning outcomes and clear and frequent opportunities for reflection/plenaries.
- The development of more positions of responsibility, including within school councils and other roles, designed to enhance boys' contributions to the whole-school community.
- The use of peer mentoring to help raise levels of confidence, self-esteem and a sense of responsibility.
- The development of boy-friendly areas within libraries and a careful monitoring of appropriate library resources.
- The use of display to present males as positive learning models and help change the culture of the school.
- The development of positive working links across pyramids with the specific intention of raising boys' achievement.
- The introduction of new tracking systems to identify underachievement early.
- The refinement of mentoring schemes, including the introduction of a full-time learning mentor in one of the project schools with direct responsibility to focus on Year 10 underachieving boys.

One learning mentor's account

I have been given 44 Year 10 boys selected on the basis of their NFER scores/predicted grades. In other words, boys that look like C/D borderliners. I emphasize that I am not a teacher and sometimes feel as though I have got 44 sons! The first thing I did was observe them anonymously in maths, English and science lessons. I did notice quite a variation in lessons. Where they were clearly engaged rather than just listening, they did well. However, they have such a short concentration span that even in one-to-one interviews I noticed their minds wandering after just a few minutes. I would honestly say that most of the group want to do the absolute minimum to scrape by; they are certainly not interested in extra work to boost their chances. They wouldn't dream of staying behind after school largely because their mates would not forgive them! As lunchtimes are only short, after-school study groups are the only real option. Parents at parents' evenings have been very positive about the work we have been doing together. They believe that the time we spend on reflecting on things has made them grow up a little bit. You do learn a lot about their home lives, how some are so hectic and some are so depressing. I do know they all respond to that extra little bit of attention. Some of them wouldn't talk at first, but some of them seem to have grown in confidence and several have moved up sets. How often I see them depends on how well they're doing. When I do see them I don't dwell on any negative aspects of their behaviour but I am aware of how they are about school. I follow their SIMS records, attend assemblies follow their Trackmaster records, give out feedback sheets to teachers.

The first session I had with them individually I got them to empty out their schoolbags and sort them out. Almost always there was work from Year 7 in there. Since then the work has included helping them with time management, ensuring they were using planners, work on revision skills and work on anger management. I constantly liaise with form teachers and subjects teachers, see the boys themselves as much as I can in social areas and constantly encourage them. The key to my role is to help them to think of ways in which they can help themselves. We set targets together that are short term, usually to do with getting noticed for all the right things. The target might be as simple as putting their hands up so many times a day. I give them lots of practical tips and advice. I also set pre-deadline deadlines which helps with their coursework.

What has really helped to make the scheme successful is the fact that it involves the 'in-crowd'. The peer leaders of the year group are all being mentored, which seems to make it an acceptable thing.

The National Education Breakthrough Programme: the PDSA model

The National Education Breakthrough Programme for Raising Boys' Achievement, of which I am chairman was established in 2003 by the National Primary Care Development Team and based upon a healthcare model that has significantly improved the provision of healthcare across the world (now the Improvement Foundation – www.improvementfoundation.org).

The goal of the programme is:

> To raise the level of boys' achievement within participating high schools, without reducing that of girls, by changing the organizational systems of learning and teaching in order to maximize the potential of all pupils, staff and schools.

The breakthrough methodology directs schools towards the following change principles:

1 Use strong leadership to create the environment for change.
2 Focus on teaching and learning.
3 Use of targeted intervention; for example, mentoring.
4 Create capacity.
5 Use data to drive improvement.

The methodology uses a very precise approach to planning and reporting change called the PDSA: Plan – Do – Study – Act. To begin with the group identifies a particular objective, related to a priority area for improvement while at the same time focusing on at least one of the change principles. The group then PLANs the steps that are required to fulfil the objective step by step. At this point the planners should note what data has to be collected and predict what might happen. The measures that will be used to demonstrate improvement should also be noted. The 'DO' refers to what was done differently to the plan. The 'STUDY' refers to the process of reflection on what actually happened, what the outcomes were – both quantifiable and otherwise. 'ACT' refers to the next stage, requiring the group to decide what they are going to do next. PDSAs are intended to be short term in the first instance. The study element may determine the need to roll out the PDSA again, modified this time, or to try new ideas to move towards the same objective. Numerous PDSAs can be in operation at any one time.

The Breakthrough Programme states clearly:

● A PDSA cannot be too small.
● One PDSA will almost always lead to one or more others.
● You can achieve rapid results.
● They help you to be thorough and systematic.
● They help you learn from your work.
● Anyone can use them in any area.

Almost a hundred high schools from all over the country have now been engaged with the process over a period of three years. Prior to enlisting with the programme, schools have been required to rigorously analyse their data and to look at comparative information for similar schools. Underpinning the programme is the desire to 'shorten the discovery period' for people by consistently providing expert backup and a rapid process of sharing good practice. Four or five members of staff from each year's cohort of schools have had the benefit of meeting together for three two-day Learning Workshops where they have received training. In addition, the Learning Workshops have included a wide range of practical breakout sessions at which good practice (largely from previous Breakthrough schools) has been shared. In this way, schools are in a position to learn about, and subsequently try for themselves, PDSAs that have brought about positive improvements in other schools. Improvements in Breakthrough schools have been impressive, especially where the nature of the programme has been positively and effectively promoted to the whole-school community. Also of great significance has been the extent to which headteachers and senior managers have supported the initiative.

PDSAs have included a focus on:

- study support for all boys in Year 7
- boys' motivation in Year 8
- holding cluster group INSET days
- a regular staff bulletin on raising boys' achievement issues
- desk mats for staff with RBA strategies
- learning/level mats for pupils – indicating what they need to do to progress
- monitoring and appropriately awarding attendance
- the development of whole-school research and development groups
- the development of a range of mentoring strategies
- the development of peer-support schemes including peer mentors, mediators and befrienders
- improving pupil movement between lessons
- physiological needs
- creating the right environment for learning
- staff and pupil punctuality
- getting the basics right, including equipment and uniform
- high-quality display materials
- whole-year group achievement days
- achievement walls
- inspirational speakers
- engaging pupil voice
- holding attendance clinics with parents
- involving boys in the public face of the school
- challenging macho anti-school attitudes
- shaping the curriculum to meet pupils' needs
- introducing project-based learning for a selected group
- teacher language
- teaching and learning styles
- revision workshops for identified boys and their parents.

The pyramid model

An unfortunate way of describing a group of schools, I always used to say 'with a high school at the top, looking down upon its feeder primary schools'. Until recently, that is, when a primary colleague said that they always liked the description as it suggested to them a strong foundation of schools supporting its high school. Regardless of your position, I believe that in many respects working on the issue of Raising Boys' Achievement has to involve cross-phase work, for all kinds of reasons.

box

Why work together as a pyramid/cluster/family of schools

- You share the same children.
- You share considerable knowledge of the same communities.
- You have colleagues you can bounce ideas off.
- There is great strength in numbers.
- What one school does will directly affect others.
- You can gain instant access to information about an individual child's or group's progress.
- You can track children.
- You can raise the profile of literacy, of homework, of anything (!) as a whole pyramid.
- The issue of what happens to boys at the time of transition is of vital importance.

In the school in which I was working in the early 1990s, we were told three things by Ofsted in the first year of Ofsted's existence. One was that there was a problem with the way we were delivering collective worship, another was that there was something wrong with the plumbing in the science labs and finally that boys were not doing anywhere near as well as the girls. What were we going to do about it? Well, like all good schools, we established a working party and began to explore the kind of research already mentioned here. It was clear that, upon discovery that girls had superior listening skills in the womb, we were leaving things a little bit too late. The practice of taking a group of 15- and 16-year-old boys on one side (boys on the borderline – B.O.B.s – we used to call them) and saying 'Come on lads, you can do it!' was too little too late. Furthermore, it seemed wholly inappropriate to be saying to our local community that we were only interested in their sons at the end of their schooling. To this end, the working party decided, within a year of starting the project, that we needed to establish a cross-phase working group. This group has been the most positive and proactive group I have ever worked with. No other agenda, hidden or otherwise, was ever present other than the desire to do well by our community's children. The group decided that the first step would be to raise the whole pyramid's awareness of the issues. A conference followed at which a representative teacher of boys at the ages of 4, 6, 8, 10, 11, 14 and 16 stood up and made a brief presentation of their perception of the issues. The teacher of four-year-old boys stood up and talked about boys at this age, 'Well, they arrive at school, barely articulate, they can't fasten their shoelaces, don't know what they need for school or even what day it is most of the time.' When the teacher of 16-year-old boys stood up and said, 'Well, they arrive at school, barely articulate, they can't fasten their shoelaces, don't know what they need for school or even what day it is most of the time,' we realized we had a lot in common. We decided there and then that we were going to work together on the issues and even agreed a common approach.

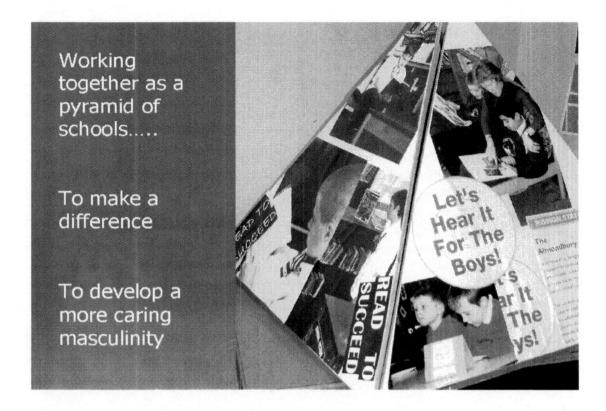

Working together as a pyramid of schools.....

To make a difference

To develop a more caring masculinity

Let's Hear It For The Boys!

After discussion we decided that we would adopt a model where each school would undertake to begin one *initiative* and couple that with one *investigation*. A neat model, we believed, as the success of the *initiative* would undoubtedly spur on the drive to further investigate the issues, and the outcomes of the *investigations* would undoubtedly lead to further *initiatives* being introduced. We were right, that is exactly how it worked.

Initially, most of the feeder schools chose to try Shared Reading as a way of raising self-esteem and improving reading skills. As described earlier, the process involved taking older boys with low self-esteem and giving them high-profile training – usually delivered by the headteacher. Subsequently, they worked over a period of time, during the school day, with younger pupils with lesser reading skills. It proved to be so successful it continues to this day in most of the schools. The initiatives that schools took on board included the following:

- The nature of classroom materials and the relative attractiveness to boys/girls.
- Attitudes to work among Year 6 pupils.
- The use of playground space.
- Teachers' attitudes towards boys and girls.
- Lunchtime behaviour.
- Joint examination of test results to highlight 'boy-friendly' teaching.

The initiatives that followed on from these examples included boys being invited to choose the kind of classroom fiction they wanted to be purchased. In turn, this led to the establishment of a boys' lunchtime book club, at which boys became massively enthusiastic advocates of their chosen books. The attitudinal questionnaire became the catalyst for a range of discussions, including a cross-phase school council meeting. The survey into the use of playground space and lunchtime behaviour, conducted by pupils at one school, ultimately led to a move towards more structured play via school council discussions into what were their preferred activities, the issuing of a school council playground budget and the opening up of classroom spaces for board games and a range of other activities. Initial explorations into the way teachers spoke to boys and girls led to significant positive debate into the role of teachers in the development of emotional intelligence and the development of boys' self-esteem.

Subsequent strategies that grew naturally from early work and which were among the most successful in changing boys' attitudes and improving their levels of achievement included:

- Those that enhanced self-esteem, such as circle time, shared reading, peer tutoring and significant whole-school responsibilities.
- Work on behaviour policies to address bullying and other unacceptable elements of 'boy culture'.
- Developing strong 'home–school partnerships in literacy' that emphasize in particular the involvement of older males in the home and in school.
- Careful teacher monitoring of the ways in which they talk to boys and the ways in which they talk to girls.
- Frequent evaluation of resources for gender bias.
- Work offered to boys as a challenge and, in short, achievable chunks, with short-term goals and short-term rewards.
- The introduction of frequent opportunities for reflection.
- Work offered to boys with a very clear understanding of the learning outcomes.

Working as a whole pyramid of schools to improve boys' attitudes to their learning was found to be extremely beneficial.

Throughout the duration of the cross-phase working group's work, regular meetings involving one representative from each school were an important feature. From time to time other staff were drawn in when developments required specialist advice, such as PSE, literacy or special needs co-ordinators. Throughout the project, all schools were kept informed via the publication of a regular and comprehensive newsletter. The newsletter was also shared across the authority to stimulate developments elsewhere.

High school subject networks

Many local authorities still encourage subject leaders to meet together with their subject officer on a regular basis. In this context lies the opportunity for a subject-based focus on the issues around boys' underachievement. One successful example of this kind of collaboration began a few years ago in Kirklees LA. A whole range of statistical analysis occurred on a national, regional and local level. The sharing of exam residuals helped to point towards areas of good practice in raising levels of boys' achievement. An analysis of various reports into boys' achievement led the subject network to the development of a simple pupil survey that focused on the key areas (see pages 132–134). In turn, the findings of the authority-wide survey into gender attitudes to modern languages were subsequently translated into action through a range of classroom strategies, which were in turn evaluated by the group.

Strategies that followed on from the research findings included:

- Making end of unit tasks more practical and useful; for example, making recordings and videos.
- Increasing the use of role play, improvisation and oral presentations.
- Increasing positive verbal feedback (and smiling more at boys!).

- Development of more interesting ways of presenting visual materials (for example, use a model or a poster of an alien to illustrate parts of the body rather than a human being).

- Using older, successful boy linguists as positive role models, in options, evening talks, classroom discussions, display.

- Avoiding sink groups of boys and developing instead parallel grouping.

- Spending more time looking at differences in youth culture between countries.

- More modelling of written work.

- Engaging boys in the actual production of classroom resources.

- Building in more time for pair/collaborative group-work.

- Presenting a wider range of reading matter including magazines.

- Increased use of internet, whiteboards, board games.

- The development of a more flexible seating policy to ensure that, on occasions, friendship groups work together.

- Experimenting with video conferencing.

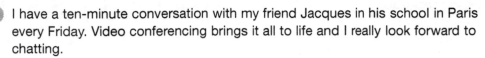

I have a ten-minute conversation with my friend Jacques in his school in Paris every Friday. Video conferencing brings it all to life and I really look forward to chatting.

Year 11 student

Modern foreign languages: pupil questionnaire

✔ Tick the box that suits you best

	I don't like it	Sometimes it's OK	It's OK	It's good	I like it very much
1. What elements of your MFL learning do you enjoy?					
Role play	☐	☐	☐	☐	☐
Listening	☐	☐	☐	☐	☐
Reading aloud	☐	☐	☐	☐	☐
Making presentations	☐	☐	☐	☐	☐
Internet research	☐	☐	☐	☐	☐
Video	☐	☐	☐	☐	☐
Using language lab	☐	☐	☐	☐	☐
Using CD-ROMs	☐	☐	☐	☐	☐
Recording dialogues/presentations	☐	☐	☐	☐	☐
Learning about other countries	☐	☐	☐	☐	☐
Writing	☐	☐	☐	☐	☐
Reading	☐	☐	☐	☐	☐
Grammar – learning about how	☐	☐	☐	☐	☐
2. Do you enjoy working:					
On your own from a textbook	☐	☐	☐	☐	☐
On your own from a worksheet	☐	☐	☐	☐	☐
In pairs	☐	☐	☐	☐	☐
In groups of friends	☐	☐	☐	☐	☐
In mixed gender groups	☐	☐	☐	☐	☐
As a whole class	☐	☐	☐	☐	☐

	Yes	No
3. **Do you believe that learning a MFL will be useful in later life?**	☐	☐

4. **What problems do you encounter when writing in MFL lessons?**

	Yes	No
Spelling	☐	☐
Grammar	☐	☐
Handwriting/presentation	☐	☐
Note taking	☐	☐
Extended writing	☐	☐
Drafting work	☐	☐
Planning work	☐	☐

5. **What problems do you encounter in speaking and listening activities in MFL?**

	Yes	No
Confidence	☐	☐
Embarrassment in front of friends	☐	☐

6. **What makes a good MFL teacher?**

Someone who: Tick as many boxes as you want

Knows their subject	☐
Keeps control	☐
Makes it fun and exciting	☐
Clearly explains things	☐
Is very encouraging even when you're struggling	☐
Is approachable	☐
Gives you a chance to get involved	☐
Is organized	☐
Someone who uses a range of activities	☐
Has a sense of humour	☐
Treats boys and girls the same	☐

	Boys	Girls	Both
7. Is language learning more suited to:	☐	☐	☐

	Boys	Girls	Both
8. Are languages more useful for the future careers of:	☐	☐	☐

	Female teacher	Male teacher	Doesn't matter
9. Do you prefer a	☐	☐	☐

	Never	Usually	Always
10. Do you always feel clear about the aims of the lesson?	☐	☐	☐

11. If Never, how does it make you feel about the lesson?

I don't take part ☐   It doesn't bother me ☐   I'm happy to do it ☐

	Yes	No
12. Do you always try your best in MFL?	☐	☐

	Yes	No
13. Does your teacher think you do your best?	☐	☐

14. When you don't understand something what do you do?

Mess about ☐   Do nothing ☐   Try it ☐   Ask a friend ☐   Ask the teacher ☐

	Yes	No
15. If you miss a lesson, do you make the effort to catch up?	☐	☐

How?   See the teacher ☐   Borrow a friend's book/talk to a friend ☐

16. How important is it to have contact with real speakers of MFLs?

Not important ☐   Quite important ☐   Very important ☐

	Yes	No
17. Do you think that learning languages is harder than other subjects?	☐	☐

Any comments

References

Biddulph, S. (2003) *Raising Boys: Why Boys are Different – And How to Help Them Become Happy and Well-balanced Men*, London: Thorsons (HarperCollins)

Biddulph, S. (2004) *Manhood*, London: Vermillion (Random House)

Bradford, W. and Noble, C. (2000) *Getting it Right for Boys and Girls*, London: Routledge

Brody, L.R. and Hall, J.A. (1993) 'Gender and emotion', in M. Lewis and J.M. Haviland (eds) *Handbook of Emotions*, New York: Guildford Press

Corrie, C. (2003) *Becoming Emotionally Intelligent*, Stafford: Network Educational Press

Creech, S. (2002) *Love that Dog*, London: Bloomsbury Press

Dennison, P. (1992) *Brain Gym*, Ventura, Calif.: Edu-Kinesthetics

DfES (2001) *Critical Literary Review*, Nottingham: DfES

DfES (2002) *Bullying: Don't Suffer in Silence*, Nottingham: DfES

DfES (2004) *Improve Your Library: A Self-Evaluation Process for School Libraries*, Nottingham: DfES

DfES (2005) *Primary National Strategy Fliers for Improving Boys' Writing*, Nottingham: DfES

DfES (2005a) *Excellence and Enjoyment: Social and Emotional Aspects of Learning (SEAL)*, Nottingham: DfES

Downes, P. (2002) 'Introduction', in Lucinda Neall *Bringing the Best Out in Boys*, Stroud: Hawthorne Press

Dryden, G. and Vos, J. (2001) *The Learning Revolution*, Stafford: Network Educational Press

Ginnis, P. (2002) *The Teacher's Toolkit*, Bancyfelin, Carmarthen: Crown House

Ginott, H. (1972) *Between Teacher and Child*, London: Random House

Goleman, D. (1996) *Emotional Intelligence*, London: Bloomsbury

Harding, C. (1992) *Wingspan: Inside the Men's Movement*, London: St Martin's Press

Hart, B. and Risley, T.R. (1999) *The Social World of Children Learning to Talk*, Baltimore, Md: Paul H. Brookes Publishing

HDA (nd) *Stand Up For Us: Challenging Homophobia in Schools*, DfES/Health Development Agency. Downloadable from www.wiredforhealth.gov.uk

Hughes, M. (2002) *Teaching and Learning of Foundation Subjects*, training materials, London: DfES

Let's Hear It From the Boys, Kirklees LEA video (out of print)

Levinson, H. (1992) *Feedback to Subordinates*, Levinson Institute

Lipman, M. (1990) *Socrates for Six Year Olds*, BBC documentary

Mullen, A. (1999) *Social Inclusion: Reaching Out to Bisexual, Gay and Lesbian Youth*, Reading: ReachOUT

Ofsted (2003) *Boys' Achievement in Secondary Schools*, (HMI 1659), July, London: Ofsted

Ofsted (2006) *Good school libraries: making a difference to learning*, London: Ofsted

Persaud, R. (2005) *TES*, 24 June

Rivers, I. (2001) 'The bullying of sexual minorities at school', *Educational and Child Psychology*,18 (1): 33–46

Ryan, T. (1990) *Thinker's Keys for Kids*, South Coast Education Region. Available for online download at www.tonyryan.com.au

Smith, A. (2002) *Move It: Physical Movement and Learning*, Stafford: Network Educational Press

Smith, A. and Lucas, B. (2002) *How to Help Your Child Succeed*, Stafford: Network Educational Press

Smith, A., Lovatt, M. and Wise D. (2003) *Accelerated Learning: A User's Guide*, Stafford: Network Educational Press

UKLA (2005) *Raising Boys' Achievement in Writing*, Royston: UKLA

West, P. (1999) 'Boys, sport and schooling: some persistent problems and some current research', *Issues in Educational Research*, 9 (1): 33–54

Younger, M. and Warrington M. (2003) 'Raising Boys' Achievement Interim Report, Homerton College, Cambridge', Nottingham: DfES

Younger, M. and Warrington M. (2005) 'Raising Boys' Achievement Final Report, Homerton College, Cambridge', Nottingham: DfES

Appendix 1: Analysis and action plan grid

Barrier to boys' learning	Priority	Ideas to remove barriers	Action: who / how / when?
1. Lack of independence prior to starting school	5 4 3 2 1		
2. Less developed linguistically on entry to school	5 4 3 2 1		
3. Being forced to read and write before they are physically or emotionally ready	5 4 3 2 1		
4. Playtimes for boys tend to be hyper physical and 'boysterous'	5 4 3 2 1		
5. Many writing activities in school perceived as irrelevant and unimportant	5 4 3 2 1		
6. Boys' difficulties with structuring written work	5 4 3 2 1		
7. Boys' reticence to spend time on planning and preparation	5 4 3 2 1		

Barrier to boys' learning	Priority	Ideas to remove barriers	Action who / how / when?
8. Reading fiction perceived as a female province	5 4 3 2 1		
9. Teacher talk/Teachers' expectations	5 4 3 2 1		
10. Emotional intelligence issues	5 4 3 2 1		
11. Mismatch of teaching and learning styles to boys' preferred learning styles	5 4 3 2 1		
12. Lack of opportunities for reflective work	5 4 3 2 1		
13. Pupil grouping	5 4 3 2 1		
14. Inappropriate seating arrangements	5 4 3 2 1		

Barrier to boys' learning	Priority	Ideas to remove barriers	Action who / how / when?
15. Ineffective group-work	5 4 3 2 1		
16. Peer pressure (anti-swot culture)	5 4 3 2 1		
17. Inappropriate reward systems and the lack of a positive achievement culture	5 4 3 2 1		
18. The laddish culture	5 4 3 2 1		
19. The influence of street culture	5 4 3 2 1		
20. Mismatch in assessment and examination methods to boys' preferred ways of working	5 4 3 2 1		
21. The lack of positive male role models	5 4 3 2 1		

Barrier to boys' learning	Priority					Ideas to remove barriers	Action who / how / when?
22. The use of non-performance enhancing drugs	5	4	3	2	1		
23. Self-limiting beliefs	5	4	3	2	1		
24. Lack of engagement with the life of the school	5	4	3	2	1		
25. Homophobic bullying	5	4	3	2	1		
26. Lack of parental understanding of RBA issues and their subsequent inability to support them appropriately	5	4	3	2	1		
27. Intervention occurring too late	5	4	3	2	1		
28. Teachers' lack of awareness of issues related to gender and achievement	5	4	3	2	1		

Main barriers to boys' learning as identified by the _____ department

-

-

-

-

-

Ideas for Action:

Appendix 2: Recommended storybooks

	Title	Author	ISBN	Extra information
1.	My Brother Sammy	Becky Edwards and David Armitage	0-747-54654-1	Sammy is not like other brothers – he doesn't play the same games, or go to the same school – because Sammy is autistic. But Sammy does not need special love for he is just like any other brother and needs understanding, patience and acceptance. A wonderful and heart-warming book about brotherly love, with beautiful art and lyrical text.
2.	The Magical Bicycle	Berlie Doherty and Christian Birmingham	0-006-64614-X	A new bicycle is a frustrating present for a little boy until he unlocks the magic needed to ride it.
3.	My Friendly Whale	Simon James	0-744-59805-2	How wonderful it would be to have a blue whale for a friend and go swimming every night…
4.	Piggybook	Becky Edwards and David Armitage	0-744-53303-1	Mr Piggott and his two sons behave like pigs to poor Mrs Piggott – until, finally, she walks out. Left to fend for themselves, the male Piggotts undergo some curious changes!
5.	Jim's Lion	Russell Hoban	0-744-59406-5	Lying in his hospital bed, Jim's worried about his upcoming operation. The doctors will send him to sleep but what if he can't find his way back? Nurse Bami tells him he has a finder who can guide him. Jim's finder is a lion; Jim has seen him in a dream. But when the time comes, will Jim's lion be able to find him and bring him safely home.
6.	Peter's Place	Sally Grindley and Michael Foreman	1-842-70037-5	Peter's special place is teeming with wildlife, until one black night a tanker founders in the treacherous waters and foul-smelling oil spills over the shore. Despite a big clean-up operation and the healing passage of time, Peter's place will never be quite the same again.

Breaking through barriers to boys' achievement – Developing a caring masculinity

	Title	Author	ISBN	Extra information
7.	Willy the Champ	Anthony Browne	0-744-54356-8	Willy likes to read and listen to music and walk in the park with his friend, Millie. He's hopeless at sport and everyone laughs at him … Until the day he's threatened by horrible Buster Nose!
8.	The Lost Thing	Shaun Tan	0-734-40388-7	A *very* unusual story about a boy who cares for a lost thing.
9.	Man's Work	Child's Play	0-859-53587-8	A board book that challenges stereotypical roles in the house.
10.	Welandia	Paul Fleischman	0-744-57735-7	Wesley's an outcast from the civilization around him. He's not into pizza or football or haircuts like the other boys in his school. So, when Wesley has to find a project for the summer holidays, he has a brilliant idea: he'll find a civilization of his own – in the back garden!
11.	Ben's Trumpet	Rachel Isadora	0-688-10988-8	Ben loves to stop on his way home from school and listen to the Zig Zag Jazz Club musicians play, filling the air with the sounds and rhythms of jazz – the music of a piano, a saxophone, a trombone, a drum. He even plays along on a trumpet nobody else can see – except one man, who opens the door to Ben's dream.
12.	Little Bear's Grandad	Nigel Gray and Vanessa Cabban	1-854-30637-5	There was nothing Little Bear liked better than visiting his Grandad every Friday. They had tea together, and then climbed up into the treehouse in the garden to look at the big world beyond. Grandad told Little Bear stories of when he was young. But one day, Grandad was taken to hospital. He was too weak to tell Little Bear a story, so Little Bear told him one instead and afterwards Grandad fell into the deepest of sleeps….

	Title	Author	ISBN	Extra information
13.	So Much	Trish Cooke	0-744-54396-7	Everybody wants to squeeze the baby, everybody wants to kiss the baby, everybody loves the baby ... SO MUCH.
14.	My Dad	Anthony Browne	0-552-54668-2	He's all right, my dad. A book for sons and daughters of all ages – and especially for dads.
15.	My Dad is Brilliant	Nick Butterworth	0-744-58248-2	Dads are special, dads are great, dads are BRILLIANT in so many different ways!
16.	Mr Friend Harry	Kim Lewis	0-744-55295-8	James has a special soft-toy friend. His name is Harry. He and James go everywhere together – around the farm, on holiday, to bed ... Harry listens and never complains, even when he gets wet and dirty or is made to stand on his head! Then, one day, James starts school....
17.	Clever Daddy	Maddie Stewart	0-744-59806-0	My daddy's very clever, he's a very clever man, he does all sorts of clever things, like clever daddies can.
18.	Rainy Day	Emma Haughton	0-552-54598-8	Ned thinks his special day with Dad is ruined. What can they do when it's pouring with rain? Luckily, Dad has plenty of ideas and gradually Ned finds out that rainy days aren't so bad – and they don't last forever. A surprisingly sunny tale about a rainy day.
19.	Muhamad's Desert Night	Cristina Kessler	0-241-13843-4	Muhamad feels he is the wealthiest of boys, as he takes his herd of goats to graze – the sky is his roof, the rocks his pasture and the desert his floor. *Al Handilillai!* But one evening he is faced with a test. Will the wisdom he has learned from his father and grandmother help him through his first long night alone in the desert? Cristina Kessler's poetic story of courage and pride of a Tuareg boy is magnificently portrayed in Ian Schoenherr's dramatic paintings.

	Title	Author	ISBN	Extra information
20.	The Best Toy	Sarah Nash and Pamela Venus	1-870-51664-8	Dad takes Sam to the toyshop. Sam wants the best toy. Will he find it?
21.	New Baby	Valerie Bloom	0-333-76632-6	Jay is fed up with his new sister. He wants mama to take her back and buy another one … until the baby smiles at him.
22.	Goodbye Pappa	Una Leavy	1-841-21083-8	'Pappa loved you, think of all the happy times you had,' Mum says. Shane and Peter often stayed at their Grandad's. There were hens to feed and at night Pappa played the accordion. This is a warm and moving celebration of life as two little boys mourn.
23.	Hue Boy	Rita Phillips Mitchell	0-140-56354-7	A heart-warming, beautifully illustrated story set in a Caribbean village.
24.	Prince Cinders	Babette Cole	0-140-55525-0	Poor Prince Cinders – all he ever gets to do is to clean and scrub and tidy up after his three big hairy brothers (who are terrible bullies as well). Until one Saturday night, when a small dirty fairy falls down the chimney and promises Prince Cinders that all his wishes may come true. Good for stimulating discussion around gender stereotyping.
25.	Bet You Can't!	Penny Dale	0-7444-51225-5	It's bedtime, and a little girl is quietly tidying all her toys into a basket. Then along comes her younger brother and challenges her to lift the basket about her head. One challenge leads to another and another, until…
26.	For Every Child	Caroline Castle	0-099-40865-1	Whoever we are, wherever we live, these are the rights of very child under the sun and the moon and the stars. A truly multicultural book intended to provoke thought and discussion.

	Title	Author	ISBN	Extra information
27.	Jump!	Michelle Magorian	0-744-58961-4	Every Saturday Steven watches his sister at her ballet class, and he longs to join in. But his mother says that real boys don't dance.
28.	Gregory Cool	Caroline Binch	0-711-200890-5	When a cool city boy meets the full warmth of the Caribbean ... anything can happen.
29.	World Team	Tim Vyner	0-099-42758-3	Right now, from England to Brazil, India to Japan, there are more children like you playing football than you can possibly imagine.
30.	The Shepherd Boy	Kim Lewis	0-744-51762-1	James longs for the day when he can be a shepherd like his father. Through spring, summer and autumn he watches his father tending the sheep and lambs. Then winter arrives – and with it comes a special surprise for the shepherd boy.
31.	I Have Feelings	Jana Novotny Hunder	0-711-21734-3	Everybody has feelings especially me and you! Waking up is my best time – then I'm feeling happy. And when we go to the park, I feel really excited. But when my baby sister gets first turn on the swing, I start feeling jealous.
32.	DAD and ME	Jan Ormerod	0-744-56032-X	This book contains four simple, beautifully observed studies of the specially relationship between a father and a young child.
33.	Look What I've Got!	Anthony Browne	0-744-54372-X	Jeremy, it seems, has everything: a new bicycle, a pirate outfit, an enormous bag of lollipops. But he won't share anything with Sam. Could it be, though, that Sam has something far more valuable?

	Title	Author	ISBN	Extra information
34.	Cleversticks	Bernard Ashley	0-006-63855-4	When Ling Sung starts school he discovers he can't do things that other children do. He can't tie his laces or write his name. Ling Sung never wants to go to school again. Then one day Ling Sung discovers that he can do something extra special that nobody else can – not even the teachers! Ling Sung decides that school isn't so bad after all.
35.	Way Home	Libby Hathorn	0-099-48681-4	This is a dangerous inner city at night and we travel with Shane as he takes home a stray kitten, running terrified from a gang, leaping through screaming traffic, escaping a fierce dog and finally arriving home….
36.	No More Kissing!	Emma Chichester Clark	0-007-13105-4	Momo doesn't approve of kissing. He especially doesn't like being kissed. So he sets out on a campaign to stop it. But then his baby brother comes along.
37.	The Grandad Tree	Trish Cooke	0-744-57875-2	Leigh and Vin used to play with Grandad under the apple tree in their garden. Now Grandad has gone, but the tree, like the children's love for him, lives on forever. This is a gentle moving tale about the cycle of life and the enduring power of love.
38.	Since Dad Left	Caroline Birch	0-711-21355-0	Sid feels cross. He doesn't understand why his Mum and Dad – Sandra and Mick – don't live together anymore. And when, one Saturday, Sandra tells him she has arranged for him to spend a day with Mick, he doesn't want to go. But Mick's offbeat way of life turns out to be very different from most people's and Sid can't help being drawn towards it.
39.	Beetle Boys	Lawrence David	0-747-55130-8	When Gregory Sampson wakes one morning to discover that he is a beetle, no one notices – apart from his best friend Michael! Gregory would really prefer to be a little boy again and, with Michael's help, must work out how to reverse this rather 'unusual' transformation.

Index

Network Continuum Education

We are delighted to present a truly inspired selection of new books from Network Continuum Education:

- Pocket PALs – a sensational new series of highly accessible pocket-sized books that have been perfectly designed to aid practical learning.

- Homo Zappiens – examines the effect of technology on children growing up in the digital age and shows how some schools are dramatically reshaping the learning experience to support our new generation of learners.
  ISBN-10: 185539 220 8   ISBN-13: 978 185539 220 5

- Breaking through Barriers to Boys' Achievement – a groundbreaking book by an exciting author that examines exactly why boys underachieve at school and the strategies that can be used to overcome the barriers to their learning.
  ISBN-10: 185539 211 9   ISBN-13: 978 185539 211 3

- Helping Children with Yoga – research shows that yoga can have really positive effects on children's learning and general well-being. This book shows how yoga postures and techniques can be used both safely and simply to benefit   your children.
  ISBN-10: 185539 215 1   ISBN-13: 978 185539 215 1

- Learning to Learn for Life 2 – Continuing the Learning to Learn for Life series, this is the second book of school-based examples for KS2 from the Campaign for Learning.
  ISBN-10: 185539 209 7   ISBN-13: 978 185539 209 0

- Help Your Young Child to Succeed – the follow-up to the popularly acclaimed Help Your Child to Succeed provides parents of 3–5 year olds with a definitive resource for giving their children the best start in life and preparing them for formal education.
  ISBN-10: 185539 214 3   ISBN-13: 978 185539 214 4

www.networkcontinuum.co.uk